Here She Comes . . .

There I was in my purple fuzzy robe on a typical Minnesota winter evening. My husband was watching late night basketball through half-shut eyelids and I was stapling papers for a church retreat when the nightmare of every domestic queen materialized.

"Who is it?" I whispered suspiciously as David rolled out of his chair to answer a light knock at our door.

Opening it a crack, he smiled, "It's Julie from the New Song Singers with the poster board she promised to bring over."

"And this is my friend Dorothy Benham," Julie added.

"You don't mean Dorothy *Miss America 1977* Benham!" I gasped, yanking out hair curlers and frantically rubbing a coffee-stained sleeve with Kleenex. What in the world was Miss America doing on my doorstep?

Running to the hall closet for cover, I waved my arms frantically, trying to signal retreat. But it was too late. David opened the door against swirling snowflakes and asked, "What are you two doing out at this hour?"

"Oh, we're just lookin' for some action," Dorothy giggled.

So what could I do? Pinching my cheeks for color, I gracefully closed the closet door as reigning royalty entered our paper-strewn living room at eleven-forty-five on a Friday night lookin' for action.

From upstairs our teenage daughter yelled, "Who's here?"

David called up, "It's Miss America!"

"Oh, sure, Dad!"

Lint balls from my robe stuck to the fur cuffs of her coat as we shook hands. I picked them off and grappled for words — somehow "You wanna staple?" didn't seem appropriate.

Finally I posed the question any woman would if Miss America appeared in her messy house at midnight.

"What's it like? The crown, the roses, the lights, Bert Parks crooning 'Here she comes . . . '? How *does* it feel to be our ideal?"

Her answer surprised me . . .

WHAT'S SO GLORIOUS ABOUT EVERYDAY LIVING?

*To Norma,
Joan Jenning God Glory
Daisy Hepburn
Jer. 29:11*

DAISY HEPBURN
with LOU ANN SMITH

Here's Life Publishers

First Printing, March 1991

Published by
HERE'S LIFE PUBLISHERS, INC.
P. O. Box 1576
San Bernardino, CA 92402

Originally published as *Glorious Living* by Daisy Hepburn (San Francisco, CA: Heritage Ministries, 1988).

Library of Congress Cataloging-in-Publication Data
Hepburn, Daisy.
    What's so glorious about everyday living? / Daisy Hepburn.
        p.   cm.
    ISBN 0-89840-313-8
    1. Women—Religious life. 2. Christian life—1960- . I. Title.
BV4527.H468   1991
248.8'43—dc20   90-21925
                                                      CIP

Cover illustration by Bruce Day
Cover design by Cornerstone Graphics

   Scripture quotations designated NIV are from *The Holy Bible: New International Version*, © 1973, 1978, 1984 by the International Bible Society. Used by permission of Zondervan Bible Publishers. Scripture quotations designated TLB are from *The Living Bible*, © 1971 by Tyndale House Publishers, Wheaton, Illinois. Scripture quotations designated Phillips are from *The New Testament in Modern English*, revised edition, J. B. Phillips, translator, © J. B. Phillips 1958, 1960, 1972. Scripture quotations designated RSV are from the *Revised Standard Version*, © 1946, 1952 by the Division of Christian Education of the NCCC, USA. Scripture quotations designated KJV are from the *King James Version*. Scripture quotations designated AMP are from the *Amplified Bible*, © 1962, 1964 by Zondervan Publishing House, Grand Rapids, Michigan.

For More Information, Write:
L.I.F.E.—P.O. Box A399, Sydney South 2000, Australia
Campus Crusade for Christ of Canada—Box 300, Vancouver, B.C., V6C 2X3, Canada
Campus Crusade for Christ—Pearl Assurance House, 4 Temple Row, Birmingham, B2 5HG, England
Lay Institute for Evangelism—P.O. Box 8786, Auckland 3, New Zealand
Campus Crusade for Christ—P.O. Box 240, Raffles City Post Office, Singapore 9117
Great Commission Movement of Nigeria—P.O. Box 500, Jos, Plateau State Nigeria, West Africa
Campus Crusade for Christ International—Arrowhead Springs, San Bernardino, CA 92414, U.S.A.

To Lou Ann,
With love and deep appreciation,
You reflect His glory beautifully

Contents

Introduction

We constantly pray for you, that our God may count you worthy of his calling, and that by his power he may fulfill every good purpose of yours and every act prompted by your faith. We pray this so that the name of our Lord Jesus may be glorified in you, and you in him, according to the grace of our God and the Lord Jesus Christ (2 Thessalonians 1:11,12, NIV).

"Why did God create us?" a Sunday school teacher asked her young class one morning.

"We were created to glorify God and annoy Him forever," one little boy responded.

In another class a little girl was feverishly coloring a picture.

"What are you drawing, Honey?" her teacher asked as she pulled up a chair.

"I'm making a picture of God," the girl answered without looking up.

"Dear," the teacher said lovingly, "no one really knows what God looks like."

Glancing up with a confident smile, the girl replied, "They will when I get through!"

That little student had the right idea. God wants to reveal His personality through us. Because we live and He lives in us, the world should begin to know a little more about what God is like.

During the tumultuous '60s, at a silent sit-in for civil rights in Atlanta, a riotous crowd began to torment and taunt members of the student movement. Wanting to retaliate for the cause of equality, students began to stir nervously. It was then that Ruby Doris Smith, known as the glue that held the movement together, whispered five words that renewed their courage and gave them the endurance and inspiration to continue their righteous and orderly protest.

Walking in and out among the people, Ruby touched a shoulder here, a tear-stained cheek there and repeated over and over these words: "Don't forget why you're here."

Why *are* we here? Have you ever thought about that?

In Isaiah the Lord said that He formed us for His glory (see 43:7).

The Westminster Catechism tells us: "The chief end of man is to glorify God and to enjoy Him forever."

But what exactly does it mean to glorify God? Simply put, it means to reveal the character of God through our lives. Though God did not need to create us, for there was sufficient fellowship and completeness within the Trinity, He afforded us the dignity of existing to bring Him honor. He molded us to display His personality and the qualities of His divine nature.

Just imagine! Doesn't that lend an aura of eternity to getting up in the morning? Whatever you and I do (doing our best at the office or around the house, loving a difficult husband, sticking it out with an unruly child, bearing the pain of a long illness), we can do it as unto the Lord! And not just for the sake of obedience. There has to be a better reason than that if we're going to enjoy victory in our lives. We must want to glorify God.

Through my attitude, through the work of my hands, in my service, in my suffering, through the use of my talents and gifts, in whatever I do, I want to experience glorious living.

My dear old uncle was a gospel magician during the '40s when Christian "magic" was still a novelty. He used to say to me (as I set out to win the world for Jesus!): "Daisy, all the talk is great, but give people some hooks to hang it on. When all is said and done, more is said than *done!*"

He was right. We tend to expound on our philosophy or generalize our devotion or spiritualize our successes. When what we really need is to *do what we know.*

Hopefully, this book will have lots of hooks on which to hang your glorious living.

> We can put on garments of praise . . .
> the robe of His righteousness . . .
> the whole armor of God . . .
> the uniform of love . . .
> > in exchange for our filthy rags!

The wearing of His glory will be attractive to those we see in the dailiness of our lives, as we reveal the designer's pattern:

> . . . glorifying God by our praise
> . . . glorifying God by our righteous living

... glorifying God by our good words
... glorifying God by serving others in love.

Don't forget, that's why we're here. We want the world to know a little more about what God looks like when we're through.

Part 1

Glorious Goals

Whatever you do, eating or drinking or anything else, everything should be done to bring glory to God (1 Corinthians 10:31, Phillips).

The Ideal Woman

All fall short of God's glorious ideal . . . But now God
has shown us a different way to get to heaven — not by
"being good enough" . . . but . . . by coming to Christ,
no matter who we are or what we have been like
(Romans 3:21,22,23, TLB).

There I was in my purple fuzzy robe on a typical
Minnesota winter evening. My husband was watching
late night basketball through half-shut eyelids and I
was stapling papers for a church retreat when the
nightmare of every domestic queen materialized.

"Who is it?" I whispered suspiciously as David
rolled out of his chair to answer a light knock at our
door.

Opening it a crack, he smiled, "It's Julie from the
New Song Singers with the poster board she promised
to bring over."

"And this is my friend Dorothy Benham," Julie
added.

"You don't mean Dorothy *Miss America 1977*
Benham!" I gasped, yanking out hair curlers and

frantically rubbing a coffee-stained sleeve with
Kleenex. What in the world was Miss America doing
on my doorstep?

Running to the hall closet for cover, I waved my
arms frantically, trying to signal retreat. But it was
too late. David opened the door against swirling
snowflakes and asked, "What are you two doing out at
this hour?"

"Oh, we're just lookin' for some action," Dorothy
giggled.

So what could I do? Pinching my cheeks for color,
I gracefully closed the closet door as reigning royalty
entered our paper-strewn living room at
eleven-forty-five on a Friday night lookin' for action.

From upstairs our teenage daughter yelled,
"Who's here?"

David called up, "It's Miss America!"

"Oh, sure, Dad!"

Lint balls from my robe stuck to the fur cuffs of
her coat as we shook hands. I picked them off and
grappled for words—somehow "You wanna staple?"
didn't seem appropriate.

Finally I posed the question any woman would if
Miss America appeared in her messy house at
midnight.

"What's it like? The crown, the roses, the lights,
Bert Parks crooning 'Here she comes . . . '? How
does it feel to be our ideal?"

Her answer surprised me.

"None of us, least of all me, went to Atlantic City
believing we would actually win."

I stuffed some more curlers into my pocket and
gestured for her to sit down. Without glitzy staging

she looked perfectly average — well, almost — relaxing on our Early American sofa. Our wooden table lamp cast a hazy glow on her soft ash-blond hair; at the same time it revealed mounds of dust on the table.

"During competition I didn't associate tasks with the title," Dorothy continued. "But after four months of traveling, filming and speaking, I can tell you that being chosen Miss America is not a ticket to leisure. I've learned that honorable titles carry weighty responsibilities. Being ideal involves more than lipstick and evening gowns."

Dorothy's humility and warmth charmed me. Sitting on the couch with a beauty queen was easier than I had imagined.

Is Ideal for Real?

When Dorothy left that night, I started thinking about what it really means to be ideal: a flawless model, the dictionary says. A faultless concept. Ideal means being exactly what one desires to be. *Is that possible?*

Most Christian women dream of bringing glory to God by being an ideal wife, mother, friend. I happen to be a generic wife, mother, Bible study teacher and camp director, among other occupations. I have moved twenty-two times in thirty-six years of marriage, and the only thing perfect about me is that I'm perfectly ordinary. There's only one way I can become ideal and reach my potential.

The Bible says, "All have sinned; all fall short of God's glorious ideal" (Romans 3:23, TLB). *All* includes women who win beauty pageants as well as women who do nothing more exciting in a day than wash dirty socks. However, the Bible also tells us, "But you are to be perfect, even as your Father in heaven is perfect" (Matthew 5:48, TLB).

That seems like a contradiction, unless you realize the Greek word here implies, among other things, that perfection on our part includes reflecting the goodness of God.

Our own goodness is like an elevator that doesn't go to the top floor. It falls short. We're like a shimmery lake that reflects the brilliance of the sun by day, but falls short of the elements necessary to produce light when the sun goes down. Being ideal can only be real for us if we become God's mirror.

Being Good Isn't Ideal

My friend Malettor Cross is a tall beautiful black woman, mother of eleven children and co-founder with her husband of the Afro-American Mission in northern Michigan. Malettor told me that for years her husband took pride in his good behavior. He was the ideal husband and father. Although her mother insisted Malettor marry a Christian, Haman Cross was "such a goody-goody, Mama forgot to ask!" But one Sunday evening Haman realized that something was missing in his life, and being good just wasn't good enough.

It happened after Malettor talked to the pastor of her church. "Preacher, my husband doesn't know the Lord. Please do something about it!"

Inviting Haman to join him in his office, the minister sat down in the swivel chair behind his desk. Resting his elbows on the desktop, he leaned forward so he could look Haman square in the face.

"Haman Cross, are you drinkin'?" he asked in a firm voice.

"Why, no, Preacher. I used to have a beer on the weekends sometimes, that's all. No, I'm not drinkin'."

"Haman Cross," the pastor continued solemnly, "are you smokin' or cussin'?"

Haman cleared his throat and loosened his collar. "With all these kids listening to every word I say? No, Preacher, I'm not smokin' and I'm not cussin'."

Leaning as far forward as he could and interlocking his fingers, the minister made eye contact with Haman. Haman squirmed in the metal folding chair.

"Haman Cross," the pastor said sternly, "are you chasin' women?"

"No!" Haman shot back, a little offended at the insinuation. "Not since my Navy days years ago. Preacher, I'm not chasin' women!"

Malettor told me that Haman's whole life was transformed that night when the pastor stood up, slapped his hand on the desk and declared: "Haman Cross, you're goin' to hell for nothin'!"

The Bible tells us:

> But now God has shown us a different way to heaven—not by "being good enough" and trying to keep his laws, but by a new way (though not new, really, for the Scriptures told about it long ago). Now God says he will accept and acquit us—declare us "not guilty"—if we trust Jesus Christ to take away our sins. And we all can be saved in this same way, by coming to Christ, no matter what we have been like (Romans 3:21,22, TLB).

God's Glorious Pattern

The truth is, no matter how perfect or imperfect

we feel, Jesus declares us flawless the moment we
receive Him. He alone qualifies us for the prize, and
we wear the title *chosen one*. Then He grants us the
desire to pursue His holiness and awards us a lifetime
supply of grace to sustain that desire. Like Dorothy
told me, honorable titles carry weighty
responsibilities. By the same token, being chosen by
Jesus Christ brings with it the responsibility of
making right choices minute-by-minute to build holy
character.

Sometimes in the process of making day-to-day
choices we blunder and don't look like an ideal
anything. With limited vision we see God's plan only
from our point of view, which is oftentimes lopsided
and upside down.

I once heard Elisabeth Elliot talk about a
meeting with Corrie ten Boom that reminds me of
how often I see life upside down.

In *The Glory of God's Will*,[1] Elisabeth tells how
her husband traveled to Ecuador as a missionary.
There, on January 8, 1956, he was tragically and
senselessly speared to death by the Auca Indians.
Corrie listened to Elisabeth talk lovingly about Jim
and then Corrie held up a piece of embroidery with
the back showing.

"It was a jumble of threads that made no sense at
all," Elisabeth remembers. "Then she repeated this
poem."

> My life is but a weaving betwixt my God and me.
> I do not choose the colors; He worketh steadily.
> Ofttimes He weaveth sorrow, and I in foolish pride
> Forget He sees the upper and I the underside.[2]

"When Corrie turned the piece over, it was a gold
crown on a purple background."

On the other side of our shortcomings, sufferings and flaws is a beautiful pattern of God's ideal plan. Even when our lives resemble jumbled embroidery threads, He doesn't disqualify us from the "Miss Eternity Pageant." He turns us around so that His glory is showing. God's judgment isn't based on beauty, poise or performance. He sees us as ideal.

How often this has been illustrated in my own life, as I grow through the mistakes and follies of daily living. Like the time I jumped in my car and put it in reverse *before* pressing the magic button that raised the new electronic garage door my husband just had installed. You can guess what happened.

Though David has grown patient with my many energetic shortcomings, there did appear on his face an I-knew-something-like-this-would-happen-but-didn't-expect-it-so-soon look. But he repaired the damage and never uttered one harsh syllable. David demonstrated his love for me when my performance was, as it so often is, less than ideal.

Jesus Christ demonstrated His love for me when I wrecked more than a garage door. My sin caused royal blood to flow on Calvary. The Son of the most holy God hung on a tree, crying, in the midst of a storm. His heart burst with love so Daisy—this careless offender—could become ideal in His eyes. Imagine me draped with His robe of righteousness and His scepter of power. *Here she comes . . .*

An ideal wife? An ideal mother? A beauty queen? Don't even think it! Bert Parks will never sing to me. I fall far too short.

But promise me you won't look at my jumbled threads. There really is a gold crown on the other side of my purple robe.

What Do Women Want?

The Lord says: Let not the wise [woman] bask in [her]
wisdom, nor the mighty [woman] in [her] might, nor
the rich [woman] in [her] riches. Let them boast in this
alone: That they truly know me, and understand that I
am the Lord of justice and of righteousness whose love
is steadfast; and that I love to be this way (see
Jeremiah 9:23,24, TLB).

I never even knew I wanted it. But when I got
it—oh, did I want it! It was a special gift from my
mother-in-love.

She was getting ready to go to heaven after
spending the summer in a San Jose hospital. One
September afternoon we enjoyed a precious last visit.
Mom was anxious to see heaven, meet Jesus and join
Dad.

Lifting her fragile hand out of the wrinkled bed
sheet, she patted my arm and whispered, "Daisy,
there are some things I want to give you."

We both realized that we wouldn't see each other
again this side of glory. I stood there, thankful for our
closeness and her confidence in God. She had given

me so much already, and now her sweet spirit was still giving.

"David will have his dad's woolen bathrobe."

"All right, Mother." I tried to be reassuring.

"Lois will want my old bride doll."

"She'll love it." I tucked the sheets in around her.

"The watch with the silver band . . . ," her voice trailed off and her eyes moistened.

"David will be so proud to wear his grandfather's watch," I said as I stroked her thin hair.

She smiled weakly.

"Daisy." I leaned over and held her hand. "You take the coat."

"*The* coat?" I couldn't believe it. "Are you sure, Mother?"

"The *coat*," she repeated firmly.

A Bazaar Gift

Mother Hepburn had been the wife of the Salvation Army's National Commander. Years ago in Chicago, at a ribbon-cutting ceremony for a bazaar, Mother was gifted with a full-length ranch mink coat which had not sold. (I guess you could say it was a rather bazaar coat.)

Try to think of the last time you saw a Salvation Army officer wearing a mink coat. Think hard. Mother Hepburn never had it on her back.

Now, after hanging in a closet for twelve years, the coat was mine.

I could tell Mother was as pleased about giving it as I was about receiving it. But part of the gleam in her eye must have been because she knew something about the coat that I was yet to learn.

Ninety-two degree weather didn't stop me from modeling my wrap for a friend who drove me to the airport. We talked about mothers and memories and gifts and givers, and I told her what I was thinking.

"Winnie, I didn't even know that I wanted this. But now that I have it—I want it so much!"

Back in Minnesota I twirled around in our living room and pulled the sleeves up so they wouldn't cover my hands.

"David, look! Can you believe it?"

He looked mildly unimpressed.

"I never even knew I wanted it, but now—do I ever!"

My husband was the director of instrumental music at a fine Christian school with a long list of financial needs. He reminded me of that last part.

"Someone might frown if the band director's wife showed up in a mink coat," he said.

That was the day I began to learn what Mother Hepburn probably knew all along. Some of the things we think we really want can end up complicating rather than fulfilling our lives.

A Complicated Gift

Consider the time I was driving home after speaking at a church in Cambridge. There was a surplus store on the way. Unable to resist a good bargain, I found myself bending over a budget bin, reaching for a wire whisk, when a strange sensation grabbed me like a bear hug.

One doesn't shop comfortably in the 25-cent bins

wearing mink. Slipping behind a dress rack to become less conspicuous, I slid the coat off, rolled it up and tucked it under a lamp in my shopping cart. When I took my eyes off the cart, I felt nervous, and it occurred to me this was the first time I ever owned a coat I had to guard.

Taking my treasure to a furrier in Minneapolis, I asked, "Could you do a little something with this? It's rather large."

The furrier carried my coat to the inner sanctum of the store and got out a magnifying glass. I could see him through the crack of the open door as he pulled the hairs apart for thorough inspection. Coming back out he rubbed his hand over his shiny head and announced a fee surpassing any amount I have ever paid to purchase a *new* coat. Just to have it altered!

"On second thought," I leaned over the counter so I could look into his spectacles, "would you like to buy this coat?" Our son was in his third year of college, and all of a sudden meeting tuition payments sounded more cozy and comforting than mink.

The furrier shook his shiny head side to side in staccato movements.

"You'll never sell this, Lady," he said.

"Why not?" I was surprised.

"Just this sleeve," he held up one sleeve like a teacher with a visual aid, "is worth so much that anyone who could afford to buy this mink coat wouldn't. They could afford a new one."

I couldn't trade it . . . I couldn't sell it . . . I couldn't wear it . . . I had to insure it . . . I had to store it . . . I don't want this coat!

Worst of all, because I had it there was no need to buy another.

So I was stuck with it. But it taught me a valuable lesson.

Give Me the Best

Like so many things in life that I'm sure I want, the mink coat ended up being unsatisfactory. Many things promise instant happiness; in the end, they're not even functional.

I really want my desires to be toward worthwhile things. But for today's Christian woman, it's not always easy to discern what our hearts should desire. There is much debate about what will make us happy. Psychologists, politicians and journalists are all asking the same question: "What *do* women want?"

The *Chicago Sun Times* reported that the women they surveyed want more progress in the workplace, more help at home and more sexual freedom. Advertisers invite women to "Have it your way!" Relax, "You deserve a break today." Spend money on yourself, "You're worth it!" They say, "Do yourself a favor; you owe it to yourself." We're told over and over what to want. The emphasis is on self, with promises of fulfillment, well-being and beauty.

Last year Americans spent more than $40 billion on personal care products, yet low self-esteem is still widespread among women. Focus on the Family's Dr. James Dobson believes that the emphasis on physical beauty in our society is a major factor in women's low self-esteem and depression. From the time we're little girls, we desire to look like Barbie dolls and own a picture-perfect home. What a letdown when these dreams don't materialize.

Marge Caldwell, a Texas speaker, says she knows what women want:

At ten . . . they want a playmate.

At twenty . . . they want romance.

At thirty . . . they want love.

At forty . . . they want sympathy.

At fifty . . . they want cold, hard cash.

At sixty-five they just want to go to the grocery store alone! (If your husband's retired, you'll identify.)

What do women really want? The magazine section of a Sunday paper featured a well-known actress. The headline read: "What I Really Want."

With interest I pored over hundreds of words trying to find out what this celebrity longed for. How she could want for anything seemed amazing in itself. Photos of her significant other and their significant baby adorned the pages. Finally, I found it. Tucked in all it's profundity in the last few paragraphs, her desire was revealed.

"More than anything else," the beautiful star reported, "I want to change."

Change Can Be Arranged

I have good news for this young woman. She will!

We're all changing. In fact, would you believe it's God's desire for us to change? He loves us as we are but too much to leave us stagnant.

Evelyn Christenson's book *Lord Change Me*[2] talks about the outside factors that mold us. We can be changed by our sensual selves, the world around us and by Satan. Or we can choose to submit to the influence of the Holy Spirit and be changed through the Word of God, prayer and mature Christian teachers. It's up to us; we choose the direction of our transformation.

Wanting change is wonderful, if it's for the right reason, at the right time.

What's the right reason? The Bible tells us: "We can be mirrors that brightly reflect the glory of the Lord. And as the Spirit of the Lord works within us, we become more and more like him" (2 Corinthians 3:18, TLB).

We were created to glorify God, which means to reveal His character to the world. As we're changed into His image, we can expect to be fulfilled.

What's the right time to want change? Many of us are dreamers who live in the future. When we're in grammar school, all we want is to go to high school and get our driver's license. Then, we get a car and all we want is to get away to college and be independent.

"This studying is for the birds!" is our cry the first year of college. "I want to get out of school so I don't have to take exams."

Then we're lonely and want to get married. A husband, a nine-to-five job, laundry, cooking . . . "What I want is a baby so I can quit working and be a mother!" The baby comes and we can't wait to get him into school, so we can have some time to ourselves or go back to work.

"It'll be so nice when I don't have to be a chauffeur. I can't wait until Johnny gets his driver's license . . . "

Wanting change at the wrong time causes us to miss the present by living in the future. We think life will be ideal if only we can have an education, power or money—brains, brawn or bread. But those things are no basis for seeking change.

The right reason for change is wanting to be more like Jesus. The right time for change is in His time.

What Wise Women Want

An Old Testament prophet named Jeremiah could have answered the question, "What do wise women want?" He knew the secret of being content with God's timing and God's reasoning:

Let not the wise bask in wisdom [brains].

Let not the strong boast of strength [brawn].

Let not the rich boast of riches [bread].

Let the wise boast only in the fact that they know and understand the Lord and His ways.

We live in a day when the pursuit of education has become cultish. Women feel they must prove themselves, so they become professional students —disciples of the god of knowledge. Now, I'm definitely in favor of education. But if we lean on our own understanding and boast in self-earned wisdom, there is a danger of getting sidetracked from our purpose in life.

Some women spend hours in daily worship of the body. It's true—we are to glorify God by keeping our bodies healthy. But we can get carried away with today's emphasis on physical fitness and boast of our own strength.

We're not to glory in earthly riches either. Some deify large homes and other possessions. I want my heart and treasures to keep each other company. Where one goes, I want the other to tag along.

What do wise women want? They want to know and understand the Lord, who offers two of the most precious gifts any woman could want.

My Two Favorite Gifts

Anytime I'm tempted to think I'm doing the Lord a favor by serving Him, He brings a special verse of Scripture to mind: "For God is at work within you, helping you want to obey him, and then helping you do what he wants" (Philippians 2:13, TLB).

Desire

His first gift to me is the desire to be what He has formed me to become. The "want to" is a gift!

Dynamic

Second, He enables me to become the woman He has called me to be. He gives the assistance and capacity to fulfill the desires He has placed in my heart.

When I discover the maturing, growing-up-truth of those two things fusing in my life—what I need and what I want—I find joy. When I am able to say, "Lord, you know what I need; help me to want what I need; and then, Lord, help me to need what I want," I find fulfillment. I experience transformation, and living is indeed glorious.

So, What DO Women Want?

An old mink coat hangs in my closet in San Francisco as a reminder of the more important question: What do *wise* women want?

The Glory Goal

Whatever you do, eating or drinking or anything else, everything should be done to bring glory to God (1 Corinthians 10:31, Phillips).

I need to make a confession. I'm an addict. I'm hooked on games. I have a fantasy of winning $10,000 on Wheel of Fortune. Dick Clark was a cheerleader at my high school—for two years before I went there—so I'm into the $25,000 Pyramid, too. Yahtzee could keep me out of Trouble for a week and a Risk in Monopoly could Scrabble up my Life for days.

Glory is a Christian board game anyone can play. Because of my dependency, I purchased it at great expense while visiting my daughter in Fresno. It's "Family fun for everyone. A unique way to learn the Bible!" And it's "noncompetitive." (They didn't know how we were going to play!) Spreading it out on the floor in Lois's living room, we gathered her roommates and said, "C'mon, let's play Glory."

The object is to see how quickly you can get to glory—which happens to be a two-inch square right inside the pearly gates square. Starting at the born-again mark, you roll dice and move your token around a game board. (If it's noncompetitive, why were we racing each other to see who could get to glory first?)

I landed on a trial square and picked a card. It said, *A friend is ill. Go directly to the prayer closet.* (To me, that was like jail in Monopoly.)

Another card said: *Of three cars speeding on the freeway, yours — with the Christian bumper sticker — is the only one the policeman stops. Slow down and lose your next turn.*

Lois landed on a blessing box. *Praise the Lord! Your closest friend has become a Christian. Advance to the nearest player and rejoice!*

More Than Chance

I didn't get through the pearly gates square soon enough to win, but I realized something. Getting to glory involves more than a chance roll of the dice.

Most people have a glory goal: Grab all the gusto you can! Be all you can be! Some have glorious goals for education, personal achievement and the fulfillment of romantic dreams. Others have gold-medal goals of athletic excellence. Today's newspaper featured a woman whose goal was to climb to the top of Mount Fuji, and she did it — at ninety-one!

Then there are those who just want to make it over a mountain of dirty socks and wet bath towels. That's a meritorious target! We have long-term goals (like writing a book) and short-term goals (like writing a thank-you note).

But some people don't seem to have any

measurable objectives at all. They merely try to land
on blessing squares, avoid trial cards and stay out of
prayer closets.

Goals are for determining where you're headed,
so you aren't lost before you get started. God has a
specific goal for each of us. That ideal ambition has
permeated His mind since the creation of the world
and can be summed up in one word — *Glory!*

Glory Is Revealing

"You are mine," the Lord says in Isaiah chapter
43. "I have created you for my glory" (see verse 7).

The Westminster Catechism states: "The chief
end and purpose of man is to glorify God and to enjoy
Him forever."

Glorify in Greek is *doxazo*, which simply means
"bringing God's innate character to light." Glory,
doxa, entails praise, honor, exaltation, worship. It also
signifies an opinion and the honor resulting from a
good opinion. We sing the "Doxology" on Sunday
mornings: "Praise God from whom all blessings flow."

Simply put, God's goal for us is to display His
personality. Imagine causing others to have an
honorable opinion of God by allowing His image to
filter through our daily activities.

My friend Barbara is always giving me creative
gifts. One is a solar-powered music box. When it's
positioned just right on the window sill in my office,
sunlight filters through the glass case and is reflected
to the little solar panel under the wing of a delicate
canary. The mechanism is triggered and "Amazing
Grace" colors my morning.

Like that music box, we can reflect God's
warmth by transmitting His song of salvation. When

we gaze into His Word, we see our image changing to become more like Jesus.

"Glory is displayed excellence," Dwight Pentecost wrote. "That infinite weight of glory could not be contained, but must be revealed."[1]

Moved away from the window or shadowed by clouds, my music box is silent. How like me, when I wander from His holy presence and lose my joy.

Revealing His glorious righteousness will lead to fulfillment. There's no need to settle for mediocrity. He can do beautifully through us what we cannot do for ourselves. He alone knows what we are meant to be. The melody of our future, the trials and blessings that pave the path to glorious living, is woven into the tapestry of what we will become.

Glory in the Ordinary

"So whether you eat or drink or whatever you do, do it all for the glory of God" (1 Corinthians 10:31, NIV).

Wouldn't the meaning of dusting tables, folding laundry and walking your grandchildren through the park take on a whole new ambiance if you could remember every minute that God is glorified in the everydayness of life? The apostle Paul's challenge to glorify God even when we eat or drink locks our focus on forever. Paul's challenge bids us to keep eternity's values in view when we look around and wonder: Can an ordinary woman really glorify God and enjoy Him forever when she's out of bread and milk?

A wise editor once told me that before doing anything we need to ask ourselves, Is this worship? If whatever we're doing is what we need to be doing at that moment, then the answer is yes. Even menial tasks honor God when done in an attitude of praise.

The apostle Paul saw God's glory brilliantly revealed to him on the road to Damascus. His unhesitating response was, "What do you want me to do, Lord?" and he chose from that moment on to be a channel for God's glory. Through famine, shipwrecks, illness, even the mundane efforts of tentmaking, Paul was able to say, "I'm glad to be a living demonstration of Christ's power, instead of showing off my own power and abilities" (see 2 Corinthians 4:7, Phillips).

God didn't need Paul to reveal His glory to the Gentiles. God needs no one. But He can use anyone. All He asks is that we respond, "What do you want me to do, Lord?" Then in spite of our circumstances, our limitations, weaknesses or disabilities, He will fulfill the glory goal for our lives.

Someone once said that God knows our disabilities and still wants our availability. When we're available to Him, what others notice about our disability is God's ability.

Glory From Weakness

In 1892, God was beginning to prepare a little girl—an unlikely candidate—to reach the glory goal for her life.

It was a foggy morning when her mama dressed her in traveling clothes and said, "We're going to the doctor."

"I don't want to go to New York, Mama," the nine-year-old whimpered. "I don't feel like going to any more doctors."

"We're going," her mama said firmly as she tied Fanny's scarf under her chin. Her mama always won.

So they walked down to the wharf on the Hudson River and boarded a riverboat. Soon after they left the dock, Fanny's mama fell ill and went to her bunk. "Is that what they call beds on riverboats?" Fanny asked.

The little brown-haired girl found herself all alone in the saloon — that's what they call living rooms on riverboats, Fanny learned.

After wandering around for a few minutes, she started singing to pass the time. As she sang one song after another, people came by and began to put money in her hand. A gentleman lifted her on to a table and she kept singing until her mother recovered.

In New York, doctors and nurses poked at her eyes. Then she heard them say what she knew in her heart they were going to say.

"I'm sorry, Mrs. Crosby. Fanny will never see."

Mrs. Crosby started to cry for her precious little girl who would never view the sky and the trees and so many things. Fanny would never see her mama's face and the birds and flowers. Her mama cried and cried until Fanny begged, "Please, Mama, I just want to get out of here."

Back on the riverboat it began to get dark and everyone went to bed. Fanny could tell because the only sound was water lapping against the portholes. "That's what they call windows on riverboats," Fanny whispered to herself.

Then she heard her mama sobbing. That's when Fanny started to cry, too. But Fanny realized she was crying for a different reason. So Fanny began to talk to God and said, "Lord, do you hear my mama over there in her bunk? She's crying because I'm never going to see. Lord, I'm crying too. But I'm crying because I'm never going to have a job. Lord, what can a nine-year-old blind girl do for you or for anybody else?"

That night, the Lord answered her prayer.

"I didn't know exactly how," Fanny said later, "but I felt it in my heart."

Years later Fanny Crosby began to understand the God-glorifying purpose of her life. Inspired by the Holy Spirit, she wrote nearly 9000 hymns of praise!

When Fanny was thirty years old, she and her husband lived in downtown New York in an old boarding house not far from Battery Park. It was when they experienced the death of their very young child that God gave her words like:

> Blessed Assurance, Jesus is mine!
> O what a foretaste of Glory divine!
> Angels descending bring from above
> Echoes of mercy, whispers of love.

Consider blind Fanny Crosby penning these words:

> To God be the glory, great things He hath done,
> So loved He the world that He gave us His Son,
> Who yielded His life an atonement for sin,
> And opened the Life-gate that all may go in.

Fanny Crosby learned what it meant to glorify God and enjoy Him forever.

> Praise the Lord, Praise the Lord,
> Let the earth hear His voice!

That's why He made us. We live so those we touch may hear His voice.

> Praise the Lord, Praise the Lord,
> Let the people rejoice!

O come to the Father through Jesus the Son,
And give Him the glory, great things He hath done.

Fanny was what some would call a real trooper. In Old Testament times brave warriors were an indication of the glory of their king. As Christian soldiers we represent the sovereign Lord. To bring Him glory is a high and holy purpose, but it's not something terribly mysterious. Displaying the character of God happens in practical ways.

Revealing His holy personality happens in the moment-by-moment dailiness of life by the way we respond to ordinary circumstances like a flat tire or spilled milk. Glorious living happens when we submit to His Lordship in times of suffering. We can glorify God with thanksgiving when we'd rather complain, with trust when we'd like a pity party.

We learn to transmit His nature when we enter the place of prayer. Unlike that Glory board game, my prayer closet is nothing like jail. Instead of deterring me, it spurs me on! It prepares me for the trial squares and blessing boxes of my future that, like a little blind girl learned, will pave the way to God's glory goal for me.

In Exchange for His Glory

> For although they knew God, they neither glorified
> him as God nor gave thanks to him, but their thinking
> became futile and their foolish hearts were darkened . .
> . [they] exchanged the glory of the immortal God for
> images made to look like mortal man (Romans 1:21-23,
> NIV).

"God made it," one little camper said as she opened her palm to show a glossy pebble. "You just never know what He's going to do next!"

King David was probably a young shepherd when He wrote:

> The heavens are telling the glory of God; they are a
> marvelous display of his craftsmanship. Day and night
> they keep on telling about God. Without a sound or
> word, silent in the skies, their message reaches out to
> all the world. The sun lives in the heavens where God
> placed it and moves out across the skies as radiant as a
> bridegroom going to his wedding, or as joyous as an
> athlete looking forward to a race! (Psalm 19:1-5, TLB)

As brush strokes on canvas reveal the sentiment

of an artist or lyrics reflect a poet's mood, God's glory is displayed in His work. Michelangelo, for example, was a sensitive man with a stormy personality. His intense emotions are evident in his sculptures, paintings and poetic writings.

Interestingly, *poem* comes from the Greek word *poiema*, which Paul uses in Ephesians 2:10 for "workmanship" and in Romans 1:20 for "what has been made." We are God's poetry, His work of art. God's invisible qualities, eternal power and divine nature are clearly seen through His handiwork—His poetry—in nature. Men have no excuse for unbelief.

It's so easy a child can understand. Creation shouts: *God is!* Yet, what has man in his sinful condition elected to do?

You can read the answer in Romans 1:18-32. The wrath of God is revealed from heaven against all the godlessness and wickedness of man. For although man knew about God, because He made Himself known in campgrounds and clouds and ten-year-old girls in pigtails, man neither glorified Him nor gave Him thanks.

Instead, man exchanged God's glory for images of men and worshiped the creature instead of the creator. Today society purports the philosophy that man is adequate, that man is the measure of all things. That's humanism—perverting the glory of God and diminishing man's highest purpose as if self-gratification is life's highest goal.

Humanism deifies man and denies God. Humanism is taught in our public schools, preached in universities and peddled in bookstores.

The Humanist Manifesto, first written in 1933

and then updated in 1973, is the creed of thousands who subscribe to its doctrine:

> Religious humanists regard the universe as self-existing and not created.[1]
>
> ... traditional theism, especially faith in the prayer-hearing God, assumed to love and care for persons, to hear and understand their prayers, and to be able to do something about them, is an unproved and outmoded faith. Salvationism, based on mere affirmation, still appears as harmful, diverting people with false hopes of heaven hereafter. Reasonable minds look to other means for survival.[2]

Other means for survival? We're all terminal! But God makes eternal life available through His Son, Jesus Christ. Left to ourselves, we pursue selfish lusts and become foolish and perverted in our desires for sin. Utterly lacking in gratitude, purity and self-control, the ungodly become passionate and unprincipled, self-willed and conceited, loving all the time what gives pleasure instead of loving God (see 2 Timothy 3:1-7).

Modern Perversions

Eight pages of a popular pornographic magazine were covered with obscene pictures and comments to blaspheme the birth of Christ. The editor used words like "porn again" and "prayboy," illustrating the kind of hedonism the apostle Paul described. Another issue of the same magazine spoofed Christ's second coming. "You've heard the story of Mary, Joseph and the angel?" the author wrote. "Well, you've never heard this version."

Pornography pollutes the family and destroys children.

"By even the most conservative estimates, a child is sexually abused someplace within the United States every two minutes," stated Senator Christopher Dodd in an address to the Senate Children's Caucus.

In Los Angeles a study of forty child molestation cases involving more than a hundred victims revealed that pornography was involved in every case.[3]

Organizations like the North American Man/Boy Love Association (NAMBLA) and the Rene Guyon Society (whose motto is "Sex by eight or it's too late") actively advocate total abolition of the age-of-consent laws relating to intimate relationships between adult and child. NAMBLA was featured on the Phil Donahue show where its leaders freely and shamelessly espoused their bias and invited new members from the national audience.

The numbers of our young people missing each year in our country are larger than ever before. Many become trapped in the prison of a prostitution ring or the lucrative business of child pornography. The proportion of girls under fifteen who have had sex has tripled in two decades, and for youths under fifteen the suicide rate has tripled since 1960. Child abuse is also on the rise.[4]

In light of these statistics, it is unbelievable that fewer than half of voting Americans favor a ban on magazines that show nudity or sexual relations, theaters presenting X-rated movies, and the sale or rental of x-rated videos for home viewing.

We've come a long way from "Noah-Noah and the Arky-Arky"—or have we? Noah's generation was so perverse that God sent a great flood.

You may be thinking about now, *This isn't exactly what I expected when I started to read this chapter. What does all this have to do with glorifying God?*

A Spectator Society

Flipping through a woman's magazine, I came across a full page advertisement for a popular athletic shoe that pictured a healthy looking couple jogging together. "Because life's not a spectator sport!" the caption read.

Likewise, God didn't put us here to decorate the church. In the midst of a perverse generation, He is calling forth a response of participation — responses that will make a difference, that will make Him visible to a sin-sick world. The creator *revealed* His glory in nature. Mankind *rejected* that glory, pursuing perversion. Believers *recognize* God's glory, acknowledging the lordship of His Son, Jesus Christ, *participating* in His perfect plan.

Frank Tillapaugh, in his excellent book *Unleashing the Church*, claims that Christians easily become afflicted with a disease he calls "arthritic spectatoritis." He says that the only cure is participation:

> What a shame that in a day when our cities cry out for the touch of Christ, when they so need our evangelical people "out there," Christians sit week after week in their pews, mesmerized by one big performance after another.[5]

The single greatest influence in our nation right now is the television screen. According to the A. C. Nielsen Company, in an average household the television set is turned on for seven hours and ten minutes a day. Women watch TV more than men, and women fifty-five and older watch the tube more than any other age group. We've become a nation of spectators.

In the margin of my Bible beside 2 Timothy 3:1-7, I have written two letters: TV. The apostle Paul writes that in the last days men will maintain a facade of religion but their conduct will deny its validity. He tells us that we must keep clear of people like that, "for from their number come those creatures who worm their way into people's houses and find easy prey in silly women with an exaggerated sense of sin and morbid cravings who are always learning yet never able to grasp the truth."

Sue watched the noon news one day while she was folding towels. Cleverly, the network moved right from the end of the news into a lurid romantic scene of a soap opera without even breaking for commercials. Her interest captured, Sue stayed with the show for the entire hour. The next day the same thing happened, and soon she wouldn't miss her daytime drama for anything. Sometimes she would peek at the next show, and before long her entire afternoon was spent in slavery to the fantasy world of TV serials. Her quiet time with the Lord, which had been scheduled during her children's nap time, was replaced by the passion on the screen.

Sue, like many women, became trapped. She began to feel unhappy with her marriage and irritable if she got a call on the prayer chain in the afternoons. Sue had contracted "arthritic spectatoritis." She forgot that acknowledging the lordship of Christ requires a response to His glory.

The Workers Are Few

"In our church we just can't get anybody to

participate." That's a comment I hear frequently. There is so much competition for our time that serving the Lord has become increasingly inconvenient. In our quest to escape escalating pressures, we pursue other interests that allow less and less time for ministry. Trivial pursuits eat up the days and years of life like a Pac-Man, until God is crunched out.

"When Christians Say 'I Have No Time,'" appeared in the Vero Christian Church Newsletter:

Once upon a time there was church staff looking for teachers for their young people, children and preschoolers for the New Sunday school year.

And some adults said, "I don't want to leave the sweet fellowship and study in my adult class," but the drug pusher on the street said, "Not even the threat of jail will keep me from working with your children."

And some adults said, "We have to be out of town too often on the weekend," but the porno book dealer said, "We're willing to stay in town weekends to accommodate your children."

And some adults said, "I'm unsuited, unable to work with children or preschoolers," but the movie producer said, "We'll study, survey, spend millions to produce whatever turns kids on."

And some adults said, "I could never give the time required to plan and go to teachers' meetings," but the pusher, the porno book dealer and the movie producer said, "We'll stay open whatever hours are necessary every day to win the minds of the kids."

So ... the adults stayed in their classes and enjoyed the sweet fellowship and absorbed the good Bible study, and could go out of town often on weekends, and were available to do whatever was good to do in place of teachers' meetings.

And when Sunday came, the children came to their classes and no one was there except the church staff going from one room to another trying to assure them that someone would surely come to teach them. But no one ever came, and the young children and preschoolers soon quit coming because they had gone to listen to others who did care about the things they did and what went into their minds.

Because we are His workmanship, created to do good works, Christ reaches into our hearts calling forth a participating response to His lordship.

A woman was asked to solicit funds for charity in her neighborhood. Hating the thought of imposing on anyone, she was about to refuse, when a youngster rang the doorbell and her attitude changed.

"Our church is having a drive for canned goods to feed the poor," said the girl, blinking her long eyelashes. "I'd like to offer you the *privilege* of participating."

It's my privilege to participate in God's plan. He has highly exalted Jesus Christ and has given Him a name above all other names. I participate when I bow my knee and proclaim, "Jesus is Lord!"

Have you ever heard someone say, "I made Jesus the Lord of my life," and then give a date of conversion? Though it's a beautiful testimony, keep in mind that God exalted Christ. No one can make Him Lord. He *is* Lord. Commitment to His lordship is merely a choice.

Gladys Dickelman, a TV talk show host, was speaking at a Hope of Our Heritage conference when she said there is no such thing as sacred and secular. "Everything is sacred," Gladys said. "Some things just don't know it yet!" It's also been said that if Jesus isn't Lord of all, He isn't Lord at all.

Three Levels of Commitment

How can I commit to His lordship and participate in His glory? Through perception, practice and passion.

Perception is the lowest level and simply means identifying with Christ. I call myself a Christian, "One of Christ's." I believe He died on the cross for my sins and rose from the dead that I might live.

Practice is discipline. Willing to be inconvenienced, to attend weekly worship, to seriously deal with personal sin, I practice commitment to Christ's lordship on the second level.

Passion is the overflow of perception and practice. It's enthusiasm. An evangelist, a missionary, a Sunday school teacher—anyone who takes the risk of involvement and exposure is on the third level of commitment.

Patti had a dream. She wanted to enter a cross-country bike race.

Every morning she threw back the covers while the stars were still twinkling and sounds of sleepy snores still filled her home. After stretching her muscles and snapping her helmet, Patti would peddle for hours, conditioning her body for the race that was months away.

Finally the day had come and gone and Patti arrived home exhausted, exhilarated and excited. She had finished the race.

"What did you win, Mommy? Did you come in first or second?" Her children were anxious.

With gleaming eyes, Patti held up her treasured prize. It was a green silk ribbon with one word printed lengthwise on the front: *Participant.*

What is the role of Christ's followers? We are, by our very name, participants in the redemptive mission of God. Jesus was sent into the world as a participant. He prayed for us, "Even as thou has sent me into the world, even so have I also sent them into the world" (John 17:18, KJV).

Senator John B. Conlan, Jr., said, "It is a great time to be alive to participate, even in the smallest way, in the fashioning of a future that can bring the love and truth of Christ to America and the world."[6]

Participation is influence. God revealed Himself in creation. We have the privilege of influencing our world Godward by acknowledging His lordship over all.

The Christian life is no spectator sport.

Part 2

Glorious Guidelines

We constantly pray for you, that our God may count you worthy of his calling, and that by his power he may fulfill every good purpose of yours and every act prompted by your faith. We pray this so that the name of our Lord Jesus may be glorified in you, and you in him, according to the grace of our God and the Lord Jesus Christ (2 Thessalonians 1:11,12, NIV).

Guilt Away

Therefore, since we are justified by faith, we have
peace with God through our Lord Jesus Christ.
Through him we have obtained access to this grace in
which we stand, and we rejoice in our hope of sharing
the glory of God (Romans 5:1, RSV).

A little boy prayed one night, "Lord, please
forgive me for all the naughty things I did today and
for all those I planned but didn't get done."

Have you ever felt guilty? I've got to be kidding,
right?

My friend Barbara has discovered a quick remedy
for guilt. You'll love this. She purchased it in a gift
store. It's an aerosol can of "Guilt-Away" and the
label promises spray-on relief from the following: sex
guilt, over-indulgence guilt, religious guilt, success
guilt, happiness guilt (that's when you don't want to
be too happy while everyone else is so miserable),
parental guilt (couldn't you use a whole gallon?),
obligation guilt, procrastination guilt (need a squirt
for that now and then?), apathy guilt and, finally,
past-and-future guilt. Just hold the can six inches
away from the guilty party and press the nozzle!

Don't you wish a can of "Guilt-Away" was

something more effective than eight ounces of rose water? I do because guilt breeds guilt.

Martha went out to lunch with her husband Fred. She was irritable and started an argument. They stomped out of the restaurant. To assuage her guilt, Martha went shopping and bought a dress she couldn't afford. Feeling guilty that she'd wrecked her budget after wrecking a nice lunch with Fred, she stopped at a bakery and wrecked her diet. Martha packed a lot of guilt into one day!

Guilt is debilitating for many women. It's an overwhelming feeling of self-reproach from believing we've done something wrong. Guilt-Away isn't a Christian product, but I find that in this age of feminism, it is Christian women who need relief from guilt. And that's no joke. We have been made to feel responsible for everything from world hunger to the drug problem. Mothers think the breakdown of the American family is our fault because we haven't prayed enough or baked enough chocolate chip cookies or marched enough on the Capitol.

We suffer from guilt for what we have done and we suffer from guilt for what we have not done. It's nothing new. Even the apostle Paul wondered why he kept on doing the things he didn't want to do and why he never could get around to doing the good things he longed to do (see Romans 7:19). Paul felt guilty. But he learned how to handle it.

The morning after I addressed a women's banquet in Minnesota, I received this note:

Dear Daisy,

Last night your message on freedom from guilt penetrated from my head to my heart. I feel a new freedom from the accumulation of self-inflicted condemnation as well as guilt heaped on me from others over the past fifty-plus years.

I raised four children and have seen sinful patterns develop in their lives. If only I had been a godlier mother ... (guilt). My first marriage ended in divorce (guilt). The marital problems were my fault, of course (guilt).

When my second husband was stricken with cancer, we heard, "Did you pray for healing? If your faith was strong enough this wouldn't have happened." My husband wouldn't attend church with me. (I guess I didn't pray enough. I wasn't a good witness.) And when he died, I felt that my prayers had all failed. I probably hadn't worded them right. I probably didn't have enough faith.

I've done many things I regret and have left good intentions undone. But last night I realized for the first time that God isn't interested in where I have been. He's interested in where I'm at now and where I'm going from here.

Daisy, last night I was able to release self-imposed guilt feelings (and those imposed by others) and know that God's grace is sufficient for all our needs! How comforting to know that His grace doesn't depend on my performance.

Thank you again for your words that helped me to accept freedom.

Love, Anne

God's Great Grace!

God's greatest gift to us is grace. What Anne heard that evening in Minnesota was how to appropriate God's grace in a way that can help us alleviate guilt. God is glorified when we accept His grace and live as forgiven women. There's no way to proceed with a healthy attitude in life if we refuse to be relieved of guilt's excess baggage. It would be like trying to clean house with a twenty-pound sack of potatoes under each arm. The burden stifles productivity.

Every person alive today and every person who ever lived has been guilty of sin, except Jesus Christ. "All have sinned and fall short of the glory of God" (Romans 3:23, NIV). The Bible confirms it. The Holy Spirit makes us aware of our own mistakes and we are miserable. There is only one way to alleviate guilt for wrongs we have done. It is a choice we've been freely given — to accept God's grace gift and the sacrifice of His only Son. There's no other way to be reconciled to our Father. When we fell into sin we became separated from the creator and no possibility existed for us to work our own way out.

In Midland, Texas, an eighteen-month-old named Jessica made headlines when she fell into a well. With her arms over her head, she managed to plunge down into a pipe that was only eight inches in diameter but twenty-two feet deep. Rescuers worked and sweated and prayed for three days before that little girl could be reunited with her agonizing parents. There was no way baby Jessica could climb out of the dark, cramped pit she had fallen into. Someone had to come to her and bind her wounds and carry her to safety, to life-giving nourishment and air.

Sin separates us from God. It's as if we, like Jessica, find ourselves in a dark pit. We can't slide back up, dig out, climb out, nor can we just ignore the fact that we're in a pit. In that pit we'll eventually die. We need a Savior and that's why God commended His love towards us by sending His Son. Like the paramedic who risked his own life by squeezing into a narrow shaft beside the well in Midland, Jesus gave

Himself to save us. He, who was without sin, changed places with us. He climbed down into the pit of our sin, separated from the Father. We fell; He paid.

Death on a cross, three days in a grave. Why? So that He could wrap us in His love, tenderly place us on the stretcher of His grace and carry us with Him in resurrection power to be reconciled with God.

> You see, at just the right time, when we were still powerless, Christ died for the ungodly. Very rarely will anyone die for a righteous man, though for a good man someone might possibly dare to die. But God demonstrates His own love for us in this: While we were yet sinners, Christ died for us (Romans 5:6-8, NIV).

We can choose to accept or reject His saving grace.

Guilt vs. Grace: For What We Have Done

Do you know anyone who has chosen to remain guilty?

I have a friend who is miserable. Poor choices have resulted in abortions, health problems and addictions. Yet, when she is offered the free gift of God's grace, my friend refuses.

"It can't be that simple," she once said. "Nothing in life is free." She's unhappy, terrified of health problems that might lead to her death and unable to provide for illegitimate children. And still she refuses to admit that she needs a Savior.

On the other hand, I had another friend. His name was Mark. Like all of us, Mark was a sinner. He lived in San Francisco and was part of the homosexual community. One day his brother had the opportunity to talk to Mark and tell him about Jesus. Hungry to be free from guilt, Mark confessed his sin of unbelief and rebellion. When he did, he found that God was faithful and just, forgiving and cleansing him. Mark felt brand new.

A dynamic change was evident in his life. As he read the Bible, attended church regularly and grew closer to the heartbeat of Jesus, Mark glowed. He left the gay lifestyle behind and with new fervor for life he began to share the revolutionizing good news of a Savior who rescues us from the pit. Many who heard Mark speak of Christ responded and accepted the offer of eternal life.

Several years later Mark married a lovely Christian woman and for two years their lives were a testimony of joy in the grace that God gives. Then one day Mark began to experience flu-like symptoms that he couldn't shake. We were all devastated when doctors diagnosed AIDS. But instead of being terrified, Mark continued to praise and give glory to God. Like a man named Job who was stricken with disease and sorrow, Mark chose to be upheld by the matchless grace of Jesus and respond, "Though He slay me, yet will I hope in him" (Job 13:15, NIV).

Mark's witness grew. He could have been overcome by the guilt of a lifestyle that left him with AIDS. But instead he experienced the peace that surpasses human understanding, and when Mark went home to be with Jesus forever, his memorial service was a testimony to the goodness of a God of love. People are still touched by Mark's story. It's beyond understanding. Mere men can choose to live in the misery of sin or accept a Savior who wants to carry us to His throne.

It's not because we have *performed* that we are

eligible for God's gift. It's only because God, in His great love, looks and sees us as sinners who come to Him by faith. We can choose to say:

Lord Jesus, I receive you.
You see, Lord,
I'm unable to respond
to the pressures and pain
of living
in my own strength.
Forgive me
please
and enter my life.

There's no other way to deal with the guilt for wrongs we have done.

Guilt vs. Grace: For What We Have Not Done

But what about guilt feelings for what we have not done? Let me see if I can explain.

A young woman friend I'll call Mary tearfully confided that her younger sister, Jackie, was pregnant out of wedlock. Jackie's boyfriend insisted on an abortion. Mary was the only believer in her family and in the succeeding weeks we prayed often together that God would protect the life of the unborn child and draw Jackie to Himself.

Six weeks later Jackie had the abortion. The baby was farther along in gestation than even the doctors realized, and a method known as salt poisoning was used to kill the eighteen-week-old baby girl. Mary was overwhelmed with grief. Between sobs she told me how she felt, and her final comment made me aware of a common problem in the lives of so many women.

"Daisy," she hung her head in shame, "I guess I didn't pray enough." The enemy of our souls loves to dump a burden of false guilt upon us.

One of the primary offices of the Holy Spirit is to convict us of sin. We become sensitive to whatever stands between us and a clear record before God. Forgiveness is as available as our next breath. That truly is a gift. Conviction from the Holy Spirit of God brings a desire for repentance that leads to salvation and leaves behind no regret.

On the other hand, false guilt leads to despair (see 2 Corinthians 7:10).

God never planned for us to bear the burden of guilt for all that we have not done. Consider my friend Mary's feeling that she hadn't prayed enough. What is enough? Is it when we get what we want? Perhaps God is training, shaping and teaching us to depend on Him by faith through the process of prayer. Maybe in His sovereignty He will choose to withhold or respond in a different way than we first thought. Is that not enough prayer? God doesn't play games like that with us.

Can anyone say, "I really read the Bible more than necessary"? Is there a person who can boast, "I have witnessed enough to earn God's approval," or "I have been a perfect mother"?

One of my prayer partners phoned me with her heart breaking. Her son informed her that he was part of the gay community. Immediately she began to search her soul, "What did I do wrong? What could I have done to prevent this? Daisy, it's so hard to be a Christian mother."

It's hard because we care so much. Taking advantage of our sensitivity, the enemy of our souls tries to make us think that the reason children rebel is because we weren't there with the cookies and milk five years ago on a Wednesday afternoon or we forgot our daily tryst with the Lord to intercede on their behalf. Isn't that burden a little extreme? Who would want that kind of a life? Thankfully, in God's mercy, He doesn't deal with us that way.

It's God's plan that we walk in victory and know how to live free from the burden of false guilt.

How to Handle Guilt

I'm going to give you three B's to help you handle the guilt in your life for what you have not done. Guilt for the things you've neglected, the stuff you don't do very well; guilt for the woman who's afraid to witness because someone might learn that she only spent three minutes with the Lord today, or for the one who says, "I know why I got that parking ticket. It's because I didn't have my devotions this morning and therefore the day was terrible." It's as though we are on some kind of slot-machine relationship with the Lord. It's as if we are saying, "I plug in my performance. Therefore, God is duty-bound to give me a day of absolute freedom from pain or suffering or challenge. I've done my part, God. Now let me see you do yours." That kind of attitude is bondage!

The first B is to *believe*. When Christ tells you He loves you and that He has forgiven you, believe Him! When He promises that there is now no condemnation to those who are walking in the Spirit (see Romans 8)—believe Him!

Henrietta Mears was asked a question at the close of her life that is posed to many great men and women: If you had the opportunity to live your life over again, is there anything that you would have done differently?

Her simple answer is a recipe for contentment.

"There's only one thing," said Miss Mears. "I would have believed God more."

We can live in the wisdom of 1 John 4:16,17:

> We know how much God loves us because we have felt his love and because *we believe him* when he tells us that he loves us dearly. God is love, and anyone who lives in love is living with God and God is living in him. And as we live with Christ, our love grows more perfect and complete; so we will not be ashamed and embarrassed at the day of judgment, but can face him with confidence and joy, because he loves us and we love him too (TLB, emphasis mine).

Believe God.

The second step to victory over guilt for what you haven't done is to *behave* as if you believe Him. Behaving as a forgiven woman is more difficult than having a mental or heart-felt assent to God's promise and gift. But if you want to appropriate the gift of forgiveness, you must behave as if you have received it. It's far easier to behave your way into new feelings than it is to feel your way into new behavior.

A woman entered a counselor's office for help because her marriage was falling apart.

"I don't have any love left for my husband," the woman confided. "It's all over between us."

"Do you want your marriage to be over?" the concerned therapist asked.

"Of course not!" cried the distraught wife. "I

really want to love my husband. But my feelings for him are gone. I just don't care anymore."

"May I ask you a question?" the counselor asked and the woman nodded. "How does a woman who loves her husband behave? Tell me some of the practical things she might do to show her love."

After a moment the woman responded, "Well, someone who loves her husband would probably slip notes into his lunch pail. I used to do that. Or she might get up early to cook his favorite breakfast. She might even iron all his shirts the same day. Is that what you mean?"

"Exactly," he answered. "Now I'd like you to try something. When you go home today, begin doing some of those things. Try behaving as if you love your husband. Do it consistently and don't give up, and we'll talk about the results the next time we visit."

When she returned a few weeks later, that woman was excited about the results of her experiment. As she performed unselfishly at home, God began to restore her feelings of love.

The same principle made a difference for a woman who was overweight.

"If I were thin," she mused, "I would play tennis and go for long walks every morning. I'd even swim laps at the YWCA."

"Why don't you act like you're thin?" asked a friend.

So she did. And as she continued to behave as a new woman, she lost thirty-five pounds!

The third step to overcoming guilt for what we haven't done is to *build* forms.

In Larry Christensen's book *The Transformed*

Mind,[1] he points out that when a builder plans to construct a wall or building, he must first build a form. With hammer, nails and wood, a temporary structure is made. Only after the form is sturdy can the cement be poured in to give it stability, shape and permanence.

Building forms relates to building a life of faith. We do what we can and allow God to supply the power to do what we cannot.

Memorizing Scripture is a way of building a spiritual frame. "If we confess our sins, he is faithful and just and will forgive our sins and purify us from all unrighteousness" (1 John 1:9, NIV). When we know the promise, God can pour in the power to make it real.

"What happiness for those whose guilt has been forgiven!" the psalmist wrote.

> What joys when sins are covered over! What relief for those who have confessed their sins and God has cleared their record. There was a time when I wouldn't admit what a sinner I was. But my dishonesty made me miserable and filled my days with frustration. All day and all night your hand was heavy on me. My strength evaporated like water on a sunny day until I finally admitted all my sins to you and stopped trying to hide them. I said to myself, "I will confess them to the Lord." And you forgave me! All my guilt is gone (Psalm 32:1-5, TLB).

Wouldn't it be great if we could market that kind of relief in a spray can?

We build forms when we believe that Jesus Christ declares us not guilty. Our faith in Him and our desire to repent give victory over guilt. We build forms when we behave as forgiven women and go about the practical pursuits of life, putting our hands to the plow and not looking back, so to speak.

Building forms prepares us for the sustaining power that God desires to pour into our lives. Released from the burden of false guilt we are free to say, "Lord, it was my inadequacy that took you to Calvary in the first place. It was because I could not be a good enough wife. I'm not the world's champion mother or the witness that I know I ought to be. But, Lord, I am frustrated trying — in my own strength — to perform in order to win your approval."

We can walk in victory when we understand that God has already given us His approval. Our performance is a love response to His great grace.

Just As You Are

Charlotte Elliott lived over a hundred years ago. Until age thirty she had been a portrait artist and poet who made her own living and enjoyed independence. Unexpectedly, a debilitating illness crippled her body and she became an invalid. Until her death at age eighty-two, she was bedridden.

One Sunday afternoon Charlotte was left alone while her family went to a church picnic. It was then in the solitude of her room that Charlotte began to feel a sense of worthlessness. She had been handicapped for fourteen years. Guilt for all that she had not done when she was able and guilt for things she could not accomplish because she was disabled flooded her mind. She could hear the accusing words: "You're a burden to your family. They have to do everything for you. Look, you can't even feed yourself. You're good for nothing."

The Bible calls those thoughts vain imaginations,

but Charlotte felt powerless to bring them to a halt. She stared helplessly at the ceiling. Muffled sobs swelled in her throat as hot tears stung her cheeks.

It was then that God brought a familiar verse into her mind, one she had learned as a little girl. One that sent thoughts from the enemy scurrying from her mind: "For it is by grace you have been saved, through faith—and this not from yourselves, it is the gift of God—not by works, so that no one can boast" (Ephesians 2:8,9, NIV).

And as she wiped the tears from her face and neck, words began to form in her mind where the ugly thoughts of guilt had once been. With these words, Charlotte Elliott built a form:

Just as I am, without one plea,
But that Thy blood was shed for me,
And that Thou bidst me come to Thee—
O Lamb of God, I come, I come!

Just as I am and waiting not
To rid my soul of one dark blot.
To Thee, whose blood can cleanse each spot.
O Lamb of God, I come, I come!

Just as I am, Thou wilt receive,
Wilt welcome, pardon, cleanse, relieve;
Because Thy promise I believe,
O Lamb of God, I come, I come!

That beautiful poem, born of grace, has probably touched more people for Christ than any other song ever written.

Paul wrote: "Where sin abounded, grace did much more abound" (Romans 5:20, KJV).

Guilt is the crushing burden. God's grace is the hope of the world.

Trusting in the Dark

But when Jesus heard about it he said, "The purpose
of his illness is not death, but for the glory of God. I,
the Son of God, will receive glory form this situation . .
. And for your sake, I am glad I wasn't there, for this
will give you another opportunity to believe in me
(John 11:4,15, TLB).

Even in the coal black tunnel, I knew the color
was draining from my face. I clutched David's arm
and whispered through clenched teeth, "I've got to get
out of here!"

I'm afraid of an awful lot of things, like heights,
for example. Or airplanes. I don't get all wrapped up
in deep dialogue with the person next to me because
I'm usually too busy reminding the Lord to keep His
favor on yours truly and the pilot . . . and the engine,
and the left wing, and the right wing. I have my eyes
closed so often on planes that I usually don't know if
anyone has occupied the seat beside me!

I'm afraid of submarines, spiders and angle
worms. And the longer I live, the more I realize that
fear is relative, according to circumstance.

A few years ago our family of four visited Disneyland for a reunion when our son returned from Minnesota. Anaheim was sweltering. Sixty-two thousand other people thought it was a great day to join us in never-ending lines where I passed the time embroidering, eating ice-cream pops and getting reacquainted with our son.

Though I protested, my husband insisted that I join the family on a roller coaster in Frontier Land. We rushed over to wait two-and-a-half hours for a two-and-a-half minute thrill. Wanting to be a good trooper, I kept one eye on my needlework and one eye on markers that apprised us of how much longer we would be on what I called "death row." We passed a forty-five-minute marker and a thirty-minute marker, then inched our way under a bridge and coiled around through a tunnel where white lanes led us to the tracks.

Until then I held my fear at bay, but when a squeaky voice with a fake Texas accent came over the loudspeaker, my wobbly knees informed me this was my cue to get out of there!

"Well, howdy thar folks," the voice said. "Sorry ta report thar's a breakdown on ol' engine number nine up ahead. But, not to worry! We'll have 'er fixed up in no time. Just hang on and stay right where ya are."

About forty minutes later, my stitchery was almost finished and many people were moving to other rides. I thought the Lord must be answering my unspoken prayer by breaking the roller coaster. Seeing the glimmer of hope in my eye, my husband spouted, "We've waited this long and we're not leaving now." Our children nodded in firm approval.

"Well, howdy thar folks," the squeaky voice broke into our deliberation. "Looks like ever-thin's worked out and y'all can climb in fer the ride."

"Yippee-yahoo," I grumbled as we settled down in the car. Western tunes blared; the attendants in leather miniskirts and ten-gallon hats danced around. (Great celebration follows repair work.)

I gripped the cold steel of the guardrail in front of me as our car clattered up an incredibly steep hill into a tunnel. Something Elisabeth Elliot wrote about her childhood and the futility of roller coaster rides seemed so appropriate:

> In that split second when we came over the top and saw the tracks dropping away beneath us we gasped at what we were about to do. The impossibility of changing our minds was an awful revelation. As I look back on it, it strikes me as appalling that so many are willing to pay to have themselves helplessly flung through the air like this, sickeningly plunged and whirled and jerked. The worst of it, the part that doesn't bother many children, is that the train isn't going anywhere. You've had this terrible ride just for the *ride*.[1]

When we got to the top of the hill and our car was hanging inchworm style, half over the crest of the hill and half this side of the hill in a pitch dark tunnel, we came to a dead stop.

Let me remind you: I hate roller coasters! I fear heights! I'm terrified of being stuck in dark tunnels! I have claustrophobia! My hands were slipping around on the clammy guardrail. The squeaky voice greeted us once more from a speaker somewhere in the blackness.

"Don't worry, folks. We've got a li'l delay up ahead, but we'll git it fixed in a minute."

"David, get me out of here!" Panic is relative, too. It's a relative of fear.

Am I afraid of death? I began evaluating my behavior as I squirmed around. My eyes were hot and wet. *No, I'm not a bit worried about dying, but I don't intend to go to heaven on a Disneyland roller coaster!*

"Don't worry, folks . . . "

We listened to the same message three more times in its entirety at three-minute intervals. It only made me more nervous.

Finally, a cowboy climbed into the tunnel and carefully unlocked our doors. We descended steep, narrow steps and said good-bye to the Frontier Land roller coaster forever.

Unlocking the Bolt of Fear

When my knees stopped shaking, I thought of other situations that have caused me to be scared to death, and how easy it is for some people to recite Scripture about God giving us a spirit of power not fear. The thing I fear most is being totally out of control in any situation.

The sensation of being afraid often gives us a chance to brag about our show-and-tell experiences of conquering fear. But there's quite a difference between willingly stepping into something like an amusement park ride, which begets adventure, as opposed to the fear of breaking under pressure. That's the kind of fear that begets adversity.

Those very real, un-fun fears threaten to engulf us a good share of the time. The key to unlocking them so we can climb out of the tunnel is trust. Trust is the hinge on the door of faith.

Trusting Is a Choice

When Solomon said, "Trust in the Lord with all your heart and lean not on your own understanding" (Proverbs 3:5, NIV), he was suggesting the choice of an attitude that shapes our wills.

Trust is simply desiring to do God's will even in foggy circumstances. Sometimes trust is *wanting* to have the desire to do God's will. "Lord, give me the yearning, the want-to to do your will." Even the *want-to* is trust.

When the apostle Paul found himself in prison, courage to endure — even though he was blind to the outcome — came from the trust he had in the one who was asking him to bear it. Fear itself became the prisoner, controlled and bound by trust.

> That is why I am suffering as I am. Yet I am not ashamed, because I know whom I have believed, and am convinced that he is able to guard what I have entrusted to him for that day (2 Timothy 1:12, NIV).

A youth director played a game with a group of teenagers. Each young person was asked to choose a partner and stand next to him. One boy in each twosome was instructed to turn around, close his eyes and fall backwards — trusting his friend to catch him. Not many had the nerve.

"No way!" one high-schooler said. "Knowing him, he'd let me fall."

Knowing the character of the one we're asked to believe in colors our decision. In prison, Paul's trust came out of his encounter with Jesus on the road to

Damascus. He had acknowledged Christ as Lord. It was settled. Obedience followed and trust trickled down from the obedience. Trust that crumbles in the face of uncertainty is trust not centered in Jesus Christ. Placing our trust in a cause, in a denomination, in a man, in a situation or in our own reasoning power is not satisfactory. It's even more than that. It's misdirected glory.

Trusting in a roller coaster car would glorify the car. Elisabeth Elliot says that full trust in the Savior protects us from our own misconceptions. It keeps us from misplaced glory and misled expectations. We can't expect anything at all from a roller coaster, but we can expect everything from the one who holds even amusement parks in His hand.

Trusting Is a Process

A four-year-old girl who lived in her family home in northern Ireland with six brothers and sisters had some misconceptions about what it meant to trust in God.

One day she went to her mother and asked, "Mama, does God always answer prayer?"

"Of course He does, Amy," her mother assured her.

Amy ran to her room and looked in the mirror above her dresser. Kneeling by her bed she prayed, "God, my mom says You always answer prayer. God, I'm sick of these brown eyes. I want to wake up in the morning and have blue eyes."

One window in Amy's room looked out over the sea with its varying shades of blue.

"Lord, give me blue eyes!" Amy pleaded.

The next morning she threw back the covers and, after seeing her same old brown eyes in the mirror, ran to her mama.

"Mama, Mama! I thought you said God always answers prayer!"

Her mother wisely replied, "Well, Honey, isn't no an answer?"

It was twenty-three years later that Amy, a single, young woman without benefit of mission board support, found her way from Ireland to Japan and then eventually to India. She had no idea what God had in mind for her.

One night was spent in the home of Indian Christians. Amy couldn't get to sleep because of the haunting sound of children sobbing. She arose and went to knock on the bedroom door of her host.

"What is the sound?" she wanted to know.

"Amy, you can't do anything about it," he answered sadly. "Why don't you just go back to bed?"

It wasn't long before Amy Carmichael began to learn of the rituals in a nearby temple. She was moved to pray. One of the ways God often answers prayer is by giving an idea regarding how the intercessor can be part of the prayer—sometimes inconveniently.

God responded to Amy's prayer. Amy realized, after experimenting with several coloring mixtures, that she could tint her fair Irish skin with coffee, making it the very tone of those beautiful Indian women she longed to serve. So coloring her face and hands and donning an Indian sari, she presented herself at the temple gate. The risk was great, but she chose to trust.

When the gates swung open, Amy moved in with the pagan crowd of worshipers, undetected. There she witnessed the horror of children sold in servitude as brides of the priests in that pagan temple.

She determined then that this was the work God had called her to perform in India. She subsequently led hundreds of children out of that bondage.

Amy Carmichael was later to say, "How could I have known when a little girl prayed for blue eyes that all those years later, from God's perspective, I was even more useful with eyes the same color as those to whom I had been called."[2]

Meeting Fear Face to Faith

From God's perspective, trust is relaxing our grip on the present and choosing to see our future with Spirit eyes. We can only trade fear for trust when we look at life with eternity's values in view—from God's loving perspective: "There is no fear in love. But perfect love drives out fear" (1 John 4:18, NIV).

To prove His trustworthiness, God may have to bring us face to face with our fears, our weaknesses, our misconceptions. He does this to give us another opportunity to believe and trust in Him.

Two sisters, Martha and Mary, came face to face with a fearful crisis. Their brother, Lazarus, became ill and died. Can't you imagine Martha wringing her hands and saying something like: "Where is Jesus when we need Him?" From her point of view, He should have been there. But from God's perspective, Jesus told them that the purpose of the illness was not death, but that the Son of God would receive glory.

"Lazarus is dead," Jesus told His disciples. "And

for your sake, I am glad I wasn't there, for this will give you another opportunity to believe in me" (John 11:15, TLB).

The Chinese symbol for crisis is two figures, *yang* and *yen*, which stand for death and opportunity. Fears can stifle or they can become opportunities to trust.

What circumstances in your life needs to be viewed from God's perspective? Is there a crisis or a fear that can become an opportunity to trust? Unknown tomorrows, physical or emotional pain, a roller coaster of financial problems—all need to come under the captivity of trust.

Then instead of saying, "I don't want to be stuck in this dark tunnel!" you may say, "This very situation I accept because in this context God can be glorified and prove Himself trustworthy."

Fear is relative to circumstance. Trust is relative to Christ. Opportunity awaits.

Like a little girl with brown eyes found out, we're not here just for the ride. We were formed to bring glory to God. One way we glorify Him is by trusting through the dark times.

Body Building Is Not Easy!

Do you not know that your body is a temple of the Holy Spirit, who is in you, whom you have received from God? You are not your own; you were bought at a price. Therefore honor [glorify] God with your body (1 Corinthians 6:19,20, NIV).

When a fourth grade teacher asked her pupils to compose essays on the human body, one little boy wrote:

Your head is kind of hard and your brains are in it and your hair grows on it. Your face is in front of your head where you eat. Your neck is what keeps your head off your shoulders, which are sort of like shelves where you hook the straps to your bib overalls. Your arms are what you have to pitch a softball with and so you can reach for the muffins at breakfast. Your fingers stick out of your hands so you can scratch, throw a curve and add arithmetic. Your legs are what you run on and your toes are what gets stubbed. And that's all there is of you, except what is inside. But I've never seen that.

Twenty years ago Dr. Charles Mayo of the famous Mayo Clinic in Minnesota conducted a scientific study. He concluded that if all the chemicals in our bodies were extracted, there would be enough fat for seven bars of soap, enough iron for a few eight-penney nails, enough sulphur to keep fleas off one dog for an hour, enough lime to whitewash a small chicken coop, enough magnesium to treat one case of a sour stomach and enough phosphorus to make 2200 match heads.

Dr. Mayo estimated the value of a human body at about 85 cents. Considering inflation, we could be worth as much as $5 in the 1990s. For me, that's about three cents a pound!

Like Erma Bombeck, I've been on a diet for twenty-nine years. I've lost 585 pounds and, for all intents and purposes, I should be dangling from a charm bracelet.

When I signed up for an exercise class, the skinny instructor said cheerfully, "Don't forget to wear loose clothing!"

"If I had any loose clothing," I pointed out, "I wouldn't need the class."

At any given point, twenty million Americans are on a diet. I learned that from a Hallmark greeting card. Inside it read: "I think that's more than enough . . . you wanna go out for a milk shake?"

Why are people so mesmerized by the body beautiful? The model Paulina Porizkova can command $10,000 for a day's work. Her 85-cent chemicals are in all the right places! She was quoted as saying, "Americans are obsessed with looks. America is obsessed by the perfect body, perfect teeth, perfect hair, the perfect everything. You know, the Barbie woman." One reporter says Paulina is the personification of a dream. But waking up can be pretty empty, she admits, "Because you are really nothing but an apple in a still life."[1]

The Perfect Form

In a world where human value is equated with dollar signs and physical attractiveness, it's easy to forget the true majesty of a man and the incredible worth of a woman. "I formed you for my glory," declared the sovereign God. Remember?

The English word *plasticity* comes from *plasso*, a Greek word meaning "to form." It is used in the Bible in references to an artist who fashions clay, wax or any pliable material. Paul wrote that our bodies were shaped by God as vessels that He could use for "pouring His glory into." As the master potter, He reserves the right to mold us as He pleases (see Romans 9:21). With His signature our worth is unquestionable.

In her book *Woman's Worth*, Elaine Stedman indicates that viewing our bodies as temples of the Holy Spirit will encourage honest beauty:

> A woman might be considered a part of God's art form, the outer beauty simply giving witness to an inner spirit made beautiful by surrender to the lordship of Jesus Christ. The woman who radiates the glory of his character is precious in God's sight and is motivated to use her body as a means of communicating who God is to the world.[2]

Communicating who God is to the world—that's exactly what it means to glorify God. One author wrote, "Man's highest good consists in knowing his creator and having fellowship with Him. God will never stop trying to make Himself known to His creation."[3]

He formed us, body and soul, to be His perfect ambassadors on earth. But sin destroyed the flawless beauty of mankind and brought distortions to our bodies. "The bodies we have now embarrass us for they become sick and die" (1 Corinthians 15:43, TLB). Even Paulina Porizkova will eventually get a wrinkle!

Two Exercises

There are at least two ways to display God's personality through our bodies. The first one is through self-control. I said that to a group of 400 women at a retreat in Southern California, and I nearly fell off the platform when a lady in the third row yelled out, "What's the second way?" (Everyone roared with laughter.)

Somehow we don't like the feel of that word as it scratches uncomfortably on our tongues. *Self-control.* Discipline. Please change the subject! Yet, there's no way around it. We can no more glorify God without self-control than we can travel to Hawaii without crossing the ocean.

Haven't you yet learned that your body is the home of the Holy Spirit God gave you, and that he lives within you? Your own body does not belong to you. For God has bought you with a great price. So use every part of your body to give glory back to God, because he owns it (1 Corinthians 6:19,20, TLB).

Control means power to restrain or regulate — "to exercise authority over," according to Webster's New World Dictionary. The control dials on a television set allow viewers to choose the time and type of information that comes across the screen. Air traffic controllers regulate what happens in sky travel. Quality control standards keep our food supply as safe as possible. Without controls, confusion, illness and death would be the results.

The personal freedoms given to us by our creator can be abused. Self-control is simply regulating the direction of our free will. When parents and staff from a high school district in northern California gathered recently to discuss teen problems, it was decided that the number-one need on at least two campuses was to help students learn how to have fun without consuming drugs or alcohol. Hopefully those students can learn to right the direction of their wills.

Self-control often means self-denial. Helen Roseveare, a missionary in Central Africa in the '60s, yearned to know the secret of a closer walk with God. The eyes of her heart were opened one day when a pastor friend turned the pages of his Bible to Galatians 2:20 and drew a vertical line in the dirt with his heel.

"The capital *I* in our lives, self, is a great enemy," he told Helen. As he continued to speak, he moved his heel in the dirt across the *I*. "May I suggest that you should [daily] . . . lift your heart to God and pray 'Please, God, cross out the *I*.'"

There in the dirt was the secret of a God-glorifying life. The cross. Denying self: "I have been crucified with Christ and I no longer live, but Christ lives in me" (Galatians 2:20, NIV).

At the beginning of a camp meeting, a man who was asked to introduce the featured speaker prayed, "O, Lord, we thank you for our brother—*now blot him out!*"

Through self-control we are blotted out and Christ's glory shines. Richard Foster wrote, "The most certain way to miss self-fulfillment is to pursue it."

Jesus Christ put it this way: "He who finds his life will lose it, and he who loses his life for my sake will find it" (Matthew 10:39, RSV).

Self-control isn't always saying no to our bodies. Self-control is saying yes to cleanliness, order, creativity and rest. In 1 Kings 19, Elijah vividly demonstrated the necessity of caring for our bodies. Depressed, exhausted and full of fear, Elijah collapsed under a broom tree and prayed that he might die. "I've had enough," he told the Lord. "Take away my life" (verse 4, TLB).

Elijah was overworked and undernourished. He hadn't eaten or slept in days and because of his burned-out physical condition he couldn't see a speck of light at the end of the tunnel. But God knew just what he needed—a hot loaf of homemade bread, fresh water and plenty of rest. When Elijah was exhausted and despairing, Satan charged in to take advantage of his weakened condition. But when Elijah was rested and fed, God sent him on a new mission. Revived, he was able to travel forty days and forty nights, nonstop, to Horeb—the mountain of God.

Someone once said that those who are mentally and emotionally healthy are those who have learned when to say yes, when to say no, and when to say whoopee!

If any person wills to come after Me, let him deny himself—that is, disown himself, forget, lose sight of himself and his own interests, refuse and give up himself—and take up his cross daily, and follow Me [that is, cleave steadfastly to Me, conform wholly to My example, in living and if need be in dying also] (Luke 9:23,24, AMP).

Self-control is saying no to self and yes to Christ.

Besides self-control, there is another way our bodies can radiate God's glory—moral purity. "Flee from sexual immorality. All other sins a man commits are outside his body, but he who sins sexually sins against his own body" (1 Corinthians 6:18, NIV).

In *Passion and Purity*,[4] Elisabeth Elliot writes, "The majority will sacrifice anything—security, honor, self-respect, the welfare of people they love, obedience to God—to passion."

Purity is promoted often in the Bible, but you don't hear it espoused very frequently these days. As I'm writing this, the Supreme Court is deciding whether or not a law intended to encourage premarital purity among teenagers violates the U.S. Constitution. The American Civil Liberties Union lawyers contend that the Adolescent Family Life Act "authorizes the use of federal funds to subsidize religious indoctrination as a means of opposing premarital sex, abortion and birth control for teenagers."

At the same time, studies reveal that one in seven teens annually contracts a sexually transmitted disease. Thousands of teens are at risk of contracting the virus that causes AIDS because they engage in risky sexual behaviors or drug use or both. Each year more than one million teenagers experience an unwanted pregnancy.

When I was growing up, there didn't seem to be as many stumbling blocks littering the path to moral purity. I remember closets being for clothes—not for coming out of. Sharing a needle meant Grandma was teaching me to crochet. We drank Coke, mowed grass and used pot(s) for cooking lasagna noodles. If someone had asked me about ERA, IUD or AIDS, I would have guessed a game of Scrabble with their four-year-old sister!

Why, I even remember Lydia Pinkham! (If you do, I know how old you are!)

Today we battle sexual immorality behind our own front doors. Have you seen the advertisements in your Sunday supplements lately? A department store in San Francisco has a weekly circular attached to the newspaper. I was shocked to open it recently and find men and women in bedroom scenes. Scantily dressed, they portrayed intimate sexual technique in the name of advertising.

What defense is there against perversity that boldly invades our homes? "Put off concerning the former conversation the old man, which is corrupt according to the deceitful lusts; And be renewed in the spirit of your mind" (Ephesians 4:22,23, KJV).

On Monday morning I phoned the manager of the store and voiced my displeasure regarding the ads. Then I encouraged all the women in my Bible study to write letters requesting a change of policy in advertising.

Will our protests make a difference? Maybe not to the store, but they will to us. I remember reading a story somewhere about a man who tried desperately to save the wicked city of Sodom from destruction.

"Why do you strive so hard when you know you really can't change things?" someone from the crowd asked him sarcastically.

"Even if I can't change them," he answered,

"when I protest and shout and scream, I prevent them from changing me!"

Bring Back the Glory

In spite of all the moral clutter, may I challenge you within your sphere of influence to bring back the glory of living purely in order that God might be honored? You can reveal His nature in this area of your life by being an example to younger women who have not had the benefit of the authority of God's Word in their lives.

Everything from bumper stickers to T shirts remind us that authority is constantly being questioned these days. Unless you and I pick up the gauntlet in our churches to teach young people about God's absolute call to holy living, the torch of purity will grow dim.

We need to do our homework and rise up and teach younger women to be chaste, to be keepers at home, to be lovers of their husbands. One church has a group known as T.L.C. It stands for Titus 2:5 Love Connection. Older women who have walked with God are pouring themselves into the lives of younger sisters in the Lord who so desperately need a role model to follow.

God created us with a strong interaction between body and spirit. If we fail to care for this physical temple, our spiritual health will be affected and God's plan to receive glory and joy through us will be undermined.

I'm not saying it's easy. Certainly not like it must have been in 1917. At a New Hampshire barn sale, I came across an old Lydia Pinkham booklet about our bodies. It's called *Facts and Fancies*.

All women who work, whether in the home, the mill, the shop or the office know how often they are not really fit for work of any sort. Excruciating pains which make the back feel limp and boneless, a dull pain at one spot near the side, an aching head and general depression are the penalty of their sex. These pains can be eased by Lydia E. Pinkham's vegetable compound, which for forty years has been alleviating the sufferings of women, making them healthy and strong.

Life was simple when Lydia E. Pinkham reigned! Life wasn't confused by Kaiser Medical plans and all kinds of trial-and-error medication. Lydia Pinkham's vegetable compound and a simple philosophy was the answer to everything that went wrong in our bodies.

Nowadays, it takes a little more doing to reveal God's glory, but self-control and moral purity will keep us on the right road.

You Can Make It!

May the God who inspires men to endure, and gives
them a Father's care, give you a mind united toward
one another because of your common loyalty to Jesus
Christ. And then, as one man, you will sing from the
heart the praises of God the Father of our Lord Jesus
Christ. So open your hearts to one another as Christ
has opened his heart to you, and God will be glorified
(Romans 15:5-7, Phillips).

That did it! I stood, shifting from one foot to
another on our green furry bathroom scales. My shoes
were off, it was before breakfast, I hadn't even sipped
water! But nothing helped. The numbers clearly
revealed that I was toting around seventeen pounds
my husband wasn't legally married to.

So I made a new year's commitment, bundled up
and battled a snow storm to subject myself to the
ultimate discipline: Weight Watchers.

"Well, hello there." The size 5 lady-in-charge led
me to a secret scale where my poundage was noted on
a card that I think they locked away in a secret vault
somewhere. (No one sees it unless you fail to pay your

dues.) Everything was so hush-hush, I expected to be blindfolded at any moment. But what really bothered me was being weighed with all my clothes on — my rubber soled shoes, my wool coat, my belt buckle. When I weigh myself at home I don't even have a bobby pin in my hair!

Next I listened with a roomful of women to a lecture about how, when and what we should eat and how to imagine ourselves thin and beautiful. Afterwards I gave them the check I had held all crunched up in my hand during the entire meeting.

"See you next time!" I waved supportively to my fellow flab fighters.

The following week I entered the meeting place positive that I was at least sixteen pounds lighter after seven days of strict growth control. To prevent discouragement, we had promised not to weigh ourselves between visits.

"But," my husband asked me, "if you don't weigh yourself, how can you tell you're making any progress?"

"You just get a stopwatch and time how long it takes to zip up your skirt," I said.

"Well, well, well!" the bubbly instructor grinned and clapped her tiny, size-5 hands together like hummingbird wings. "Now comes the part we've all been waiting for."

I stepped onto the scales and felt totally humiliated and defeated and deflated as she squealed with delight, "Oh, Daisy, dear! You've lost one and one-fourth pounds! That's great!" (No one noticed that I had come without my coat.) She clapped some more and fluttered into the group room to address the other clients.

I wrote another check.

"Ladies! L*adees*!" our leader called the meeting to order. "I always like to start our evenings by reporting and celebrating how much weight our entire group has lost." A holy hush fell over the room.

"All together you girls have dropped twelve and one-half pounds!"

We all clapped like hummingbird wings because we wanted to follow our size-5 leader.

"And our newest member," she pinched her lips together, squinted her eyes and then clicked her tongue in approval, "Daisy . . . has lost . . . " she paused breathlessly for dramatic effect. I slid down in my chair. " . . . one and one-fourth pounds!" Clapclapclapclapclapclap!

When I put my check on the desk that night, I decided that it should be against the law to wear a size 5. And as I subtracted the check amount from my not-too-impressive bank balance, I asked myself: *Why am I spending perfectly good money to have someone tell me what I should eat and drink and how I should behave, when I already know those things full well?*

I continued to think about it as I drove home. Didn't I have the discipline, the willpower, to bring my body under subjection? Of course I did! After all, the Lord and I can do anything together.

I pulled into the driveway, picked up the evening paper and walked into my cozy kitchen where I poured a cup of coffee — no cream and sugar, because the size-5 lady said so.

As I leafed through the newspaper, my eyes fell upon a section labeled *Support Groups for Women*. I had never really noticed before, but the number of women's support groups was astounding!

Mastectomy assistance, single mothers, abused wives, women with low self-esteem, women with weight problems and drug problems. The list went on and on. There was even a generic group for women who might like support and counseling on any issue they could think of. Suddenly I realized something that hadn't occurred to me until that moment: There is a basic, intense, God-given need built right in to every human being—the need for encouragement.

We *need* a support system. Those who will cheer us on and say, "You can do it!" Those who will give us a warm hug and remind us, "You can make it!"

The well-attended weight loss class illustrated my point. *The need for encouragement is so overwhelming, we're even willing to pay for it.* But friendly support means so much more when given freely from someone who knows and cares about our personal struggles.

A little boy asked his busy mom, "Can we play darts now?" "Sure, Honey," she said, wanting to encourage him to use his new birthday present. "We'll take turns throwing." "Oh, no. I didn't mean that," the five-year-old said. "I'll throw. You just watch me and say *wonderful!*"

The Bible says, "Let us consider how we may spur one another on ... let us not give up meeting together ... but let us encourage one another—and all the more as you see the Day approaching" (Hebrews 10:24,25, NIV).

The Three Parts to Encouragement

Encouragement is a three-part word:

1. *En* is a prefix meaning "to cover or surround with; to place into; to give as a gift."

2. *Courage* means "bravery," of course. It's the ability to meet danger or opposition with calmness and firmness. Courage is fearlessness.

3. *Ment* is the "result of something which has occurred."

Life brings plenty of opposition. What we need is people who will help us face life bravely. Sometimes we need a friend who will sandwich the courage between *en* and *ment* — giving us a reason to hang on just for today. Someone who will observe our efforts and say *wonderful* as they cheer us on.

We glorify God when we become the encourager to someone else. When Paul was blinded on the road to Damascus, his world turned upside down — He met Jesus. No longer could he persecute those who followed Christ because now he was one of them.

But criticism and discouragement greeted him at every turn. Who would believe him after his past life? The disciples were suspicious and he knew it.

Then Barnabas came along. He was willing to stand by in the face of opposition and encourage Paul to continue in ministry. Barnabas spoke to the other disciples on Paul's behalf. He believed in him. Barnabas gave Paul the gift of bravery. And Paul became the greatest evangelist of his day. He had the courage to open his heart to the Holy Spirit who used him to write a large portion of the New Testament.

Barnabas not only supported Paul, but he was also sent to the church in Antioch. "He was glad and encouraged them all to remain true to the Lord with all their hearts . . . and a great number of people were brought to the Lord" (Acts 11:23,24, NIV). Then he went to Tarsus, found Paul and together for one year they encouraged the Antioch believers.

So important was his ministry, Barnabas was referred to as the son of encouragement. That was his friends' way of saying when you look up the word *encouragement* in the dictionary, you'll find a picture of Barnabas! The people at Antioch learned that good fruit is always the result of encouragement.

Encouragement is helping others face life bravely. Encouragement is love acted out. The following words were posted in my daughter's college room: "Love talked about is easily turned aside but love demonstrated is irresistible."

Love searches for ways to express itself. That's encouragement. Ask not what another can do for you. Ask what you can do for another.

> May the God who inspires men to endure, and gives them a father's care, give you a mind united toward one another because of your common loyalty to Jesus Christ. And then, as one man, you will sing from the heart the praises of God the Father of our Lord Jesus Christ. So open your hearts to one another as Christ has opened his heart to you, and God will be glorified (Romans 15:5-7, Phillips).

Encouragement is opening our hearts to others. It's being united. Encouragement is moving in and out of each others' lives, not to discourage and criticize but to build up. Then others glorify God because of what they see in us.

"Therefore encourage one another and build each other up, just as in fact you are doing" (1 Thessalonians 5:11, NIV).

Five Ways to Become a Barnabas

Here are some practical ways to cultivate a spirit of encouragement in your life:

Cancel Criticism

Two junior highers were talking on the school recreation field about a classmate.

"She's no good at volleyball," one of them remarked.

The other girl quickly responded, "Yeah, but she always tries her best."

The critical one added, "She's not very smart in school either."

"Maybe so," her friend answered. "But I know she studies hard. It's not as easy for her to get good grades as it is for you."

Determined to sway her friend's opinion to her way of seeing things, the exasperated youth sneered, "Did you ever notice how ragged her clothes are? They're really out of style. I think they're ugly."

"Yes, but have you noticed how clean they always are?"[1]

The Bible reminds us to look for things that are worthy of praise in others, things that will cancel out the criticism (see Philippians 4:8). When you're tempted to see the worst in someone, search for the best.

> You are building up or tearing down
>   no matter what you do.
> So choose to work with the construction gang
>   and not the wrecking crew!
>
>   —Anonymous

Play Second Fiddle

Leonard Bernstein was asked by an admirer, "Mr. Bernstein, what is the most difficult instrument to play?"

"Second fiddle," he answered without hesitation. "I can get plenty of first violinists, but to find someone who plays second violin to support the melody—now that's a problem!"

The Bible gives us word pictures that describe how we can be supportive of others instead of just looking to our own interests:

> But God is faithful [to His Word and to his compassionate nature], and He [can be trusted] not to let you be tempted and tried and assayed beyond your ability and strength of resistance and power to endure, but with the temptation He will [always] also provide the way out—the means to escape to a *landing place*—that you may be capable and strong and powerful patiently to bear up under it (1 Corinthians 10:13, AMP, italics mine).

If you've ever been in an airplane on a foggy day or in the middle of the night, you know how good a lighted runway looks. In our daily lives, we can be landing places for each other, the lighted runway for a friend flying in the fog.

When the demands of the world make you feel like you're playing solo when the music calls for a duet, come to me for support. That's what the Bible teaches us. God has given us to each other for that reason. Don't let your friends fiddle around all alone.

Dear Lord,
You know I'm willing
    to be a soloist for You

> Though it's frightening sometimes,
> it's fun, too.
> Being on stage
> Being the center of attention
> Feeling your power flow through me.
> But there are times
> You give the leading role
> to another
> and I must sing harmony.
> Supporting, following,
> praying that You'll shine
> through someone else and get glory
> when the task is complete.
> Help me, Lord
> to put my own ambitions aside
> to be an encourager
> to build others up
> to play the accompaniment
> in Your song of praise
> for your glory. Amen.

Choose Joy

A few years ago I found myself in a remote camping area in Canada with 100 women and at least 2000 mosquitos. It rained and rained, making the campsite a mud bowl. To top everything off I had picked up a parasite somewhere along the way (but didn't realize yet that it was the cause of my illness).

I would get myself up and speak at one of the sessions, then go back to bed and die a little. A few hours later I'd drag myself back to another meeting, return to my quarters and collapse.

"Lord, I'm not gonna make it," I prayed. "And besides that, Lord, I don't *want* to make it!"

If only it would stop raining, I thought, maybe the mud, mosquitos and humidity wouldn't be so bad.

My depressed attitude was checked when an

unimposing little grandmotherly lady with silver hair and wire spectacles shared this quip:

> It hain't no use to grumble and complain.
> It's just as cheap and easy to rejoice.
> When God sorts out the weather and sends rain,
> Then . . . rain's MY choice!

I can choose my attitude!

Envy . . . or . . . Enthusiasm

Greed . . . or . . . Gratitude

Belief . . . or . . . Bitterness

Stress . . . or . . . Serenity

Pouting . . . or . . . Praising

Complaining . . . or . . . Contentment.

That which I choose will affect those around me. My attitude has the power to discourage or encourage others.

From Elisabeth Elliot's recent newsletter, here are eight discouraging ways to make yourself (and quite a few others) miserable:

1. Count your troubles, name them one by one—at the breakfast table, if anybody will listen, or as soon as possible thereafter.

2. Worry every day about something. Don't let yourself get out of practice. It won't add a cubit to your stature but it might burn a few calories.

3. Pity yourself. If you do enough of this, nobody else will have to do it for you.

4. Make sure you get your rights. Never mind

other people's. You have your life to live; they have theirs.

5. Don't fall into any compassion traps—the sort of situation where people can walk all over you. If you get too involved in other people's troubles, you may neglect your own.

6. Be right, and be sure to let folks know about it. If you catch yourself in the wrong, don't breathe it to a soul.

7. Review daily the names of people who have hurt, wronged or insulted you. Keep those lists up to date, and think of ways to get even without being thought of as unreasonable, uncivilized or unChristian.

8. Never forgive a wrong. Clutch it forever, and you'll never be unemployed. Resentment is a full-time job.

Do you want to be a Barnabas? Then choose joy! Be positive and resist the urge to see only the negatives in life.

If you keep on saying things are going to be bad— you have a good chance of being a prophet.

In the long run the pessimist might be proved right, but the optimist has a better time on the trip!

Cultivate a Cheerful Countenance

Your countenance counts!

Many years ago a small band of prospectors hiked into the mountains of Montana to seek their fortune. Shortly after they set up camp and began digging in the rocky soil, they struck gold.

When the need arose for food and supplies, two

of the men were sent down the mountain to a nearby village.

"Don't tell a soul about our discovery," the oldest miner warned, as they started off on their journey.

Several days later when the men returned with sacks of flour, coffee and dried goods, they were followed by scores of townspeople.

Disgusted that he couldn't trust his partners, the old prospector pulled aside one from the crowd.

"Which of my friends told you about our find?" he asked.

"Neither one," said the fellow. "We could tell by the look on their faces."

Can people tell by the look on your face that you've discovered a wonderful relationship with the Savior?

"We Christians have no veil over our faces: we can be mirrors that brightly reflect the glory of the Lord. And as the Spirit of the Lord works with us, we become more and more like him" (2 Corinthians 3:18, TLB).

Reverend Oliver Wilson once said, "Laughter is God's hand on a troubled world."

Nehemiah told his people that the joy of the Lord was their strength (see 8:10). When you radiate joy it is a great sense of strength and encouragement to others. Those around you can sense that you care for them. Your countenance conveys a message: "Be encouraged! You can make it!"

Cultivating a healthy countenance lets others know you think they're special. Someone has said:

We are not what we think we are . . .

We are not even what others think we are . . .

We are what we think others think we are.[2]

You can be a steward of God's love for others. To the clerk in the grocery store who's had a bad day, to the neighbor who just moved to town, to the little girl selling cookies at your door—you can be a steward of God's love for them just by the look on your face. Remember, your countenance counts!

My friend Winnie says that by the time you're fifty you have the face you deserve! How's your face? Is it getting bitter or better? Is it showing the signs of a glowing, growing relationship with the Lord of all joy and peace?

> Lord, give me courage to live!
> A cheerful courage, Master, if possible.
> Let me wear a smile even when my heart trembles:
> let laughter-lines form around my eyes,
> and let me hold my chin up and go forward.
>
> —Flora Larsson[3]

Coin Praise Phrases Daily

At the breakfast table a husband read something from the newspaper to his grumpy wife: "According to new statistics, the average woman spends two hours a day feeling discouraged, depressed or insecure."

"Well, what do you know!" the woman exclaimed. "I'm finally above average in something!"

Many people desperately need to feel that they are significant. A single sentence or phrase can do wonders to boost someone's sense of self-worth.

"You're special to me."

"I'm so glad you're my neighbor!"

"Thank you for being you."

"What would I do without you?"

"The Lord was good when He gave me you!"

Isn't that simple? Why not invent some of your own encouragement phrases and make a commitment to deliver at least one a day. At one church "encouragement cards" are placed in the pew racks every Sunday. They're just blank index cards where each person is asked to write a note of loving encouragement to someone in the congregation. The cards are collected in the offering place and mailed out from the church office. What an upper!

Erma Bombeck mails herself encouragement cards while she's on vacation having a terrific time. She says that after doing laundry for three solid days, cleaning out the green furry things in the refrigerator and paying $80 to get the dog out of the kennel, the postcards she sends herself really help.

Good News/Bad News

Learning to give others the gift of courage is essential as we move in and out of the storms of life.

Paul was taken prisoner and forced aboard a ship destined for Asia, where he would stand trial before Caesar. It seemed to Paul that the pilot and ship owner had picked a terrible time to sail. It was winter when hurricane winds tossed the seas.

"Men, our voyage is going to be disastrous," Paul warned.

But who would listen to a prisoner?

Sure enough, it wasn't long before the dangerous "Northeaster" swept down from Crete. The ship was tossed and badgered by ferocious waves and the sailors gave up hope. Cargo was tossed overboard in an effort to lighten the ship. The crew had gone a long time without food and would have probably perished from starvation and exposure if it hadn't been for Paul's encouragement.

He stood before them and first took the opportunity to say, "I told you so."

"Men, you should have taken my advice not to sail from Crete: then you would have spared yourselves this damage and loss" (Acts 27:21, NIV).

As if they didn't already realize that!

Then he followed with words of comfort: "I urge you to keep up your courage" (verse 22).

Because Paul had such a close walk with the Lord, he was sensitive to the message sent by an angel the night before.

"Don't be afraid!" the angel encouraged Paul and he was able to help the others face life bravely.

As is often the case, Paul had good news and bad news.

"I urge you to keep up your courage, because not one of you will be lost: only the ship will be destroyed" (verse 22).

The good news is: You're going to make it!

The bad news is: You may not have much to hang on to.

Don't you feel like that sometimes? You've been through storms before and God always sees you through. You know He will again. But it often feels like the bottom has dropped out, like there's not much to hang on to.

Then Paul followed with some practical advice: "For the last fourteen days, you have been in constant suspense and have gone without food—you haven't eaten anything. Now I urge you to take some food. You need it to survive" (verses 33,34).

There's never been a time in my life when I was too nervous to eat! I'm glad to discover that it's scriptural to "take some food." When I know someone is going through one of life's storms, I try to invite them over for lunch. (We always check our Weight Watchers' menus.) We celebrate the fact that we've made it this far and ask God to strengthen us for the road ahead.

Paul took some bread and gave thanks to God in front of all the men. Then he broke it and began to eat. The Bible says, "They were all encouraged and ate some themselves" (verse 36).

What those discouraged fellows needed was a life raft, something to hang on to. They had cut the ropes to their life boat and had even thrown the ship's tackle overboard. There seemed to be nothing left to hope in. It was Paul's positive attitude, his cheerful optimistic countenance, his praise phrases that pulled them through. Paul became a life raft. And although the ship struck a sandbar and was broken into pieces, every man lived.

When you and I concentrate on becoming an encourager, we are life rafts to those facing big storms. We can give thanks to God in their stead. We can pass along a message of hope. We can even prepare a banquet and strengthen them for the tumultuous journey.

Lord, I've been feeling so discouraged —
    so depressed.
I've been filled with so many self-doubts
    and so many feelings of inadequacy and
    worthlessness.

Thank You, Lord, for knowing and understanding
    my mixed-up feelings:
    and for caring so much that

You placed my unexpressed needs on a
friend's heart.

Thank You for my friend's sensitivity to Your leading.
Thank You that she took the time to pray earnestly
for me.

Thank You that she was obedient
to your prompting her to call me.

Thank You, Lord, for giving her the words of
reassurance and affirmation
encouragement and hope
that I needed to hear.

Thank You for her praying with me over the phone,
and for the way Your love touched me
anew through her prayer.

Lord, let me learn from this
to be obedient and responsive to Your inner
promptings—
to those times when You would use me to
bring Your words of encouragement, hope
and love to someone who is hurting.

"But exhort [encourage] one another day after day"
(Hebrews 3:13).

                    —Marlene Bagnull[4]

Gift Exchange

Serve one another with the particular gifts God has
given each of you, as faithful dispensers of the
magnificently varied grace of God . . . And in whatever
way a man serves the Church he should do it
recognizing the fact that God gives him his ability, so
that God may be glorified in everything through Jesus
Christ (1 Peter 4:10,11, Phillips).

"Grandma, were you on Noah's ark?" asked
five-year-old Jennifer.

"Of course not!" her grandma responded.

"Then," Jennifer's eyes widened with wonder,
"why weren't you drowned?"

I was as surprised as Jennifer's grandma the first
time a waitress handed me a senior citizen's menu.
My friend gave me this quip to ease the transition
from freckles to age spots:

How do I know my youth is all spent?
My get-up-and-go has got up and went.
But in spite of it all I am able to grin
When I think of the places my get-up has been!

A Lesson From Gifts

Even though age is not often the favorite subject

of a prime-timer, I love birthdays. I'm a party person. My motto is: Until further notice—*Celebrate!* I love to kick up my heels and laugh and give surprise presents, but most of all I love to receive gifts!

On my birthday, when Lois was sixteen (notice whose age I mentioned), she planned a party for me. My daughter was working long hours after school at a beauty parlor, but she took time to bake a cake, decorate our kitchen and wrap presents. It meant a lot that Lois spent her precious free time to please me.

At the birthday party my loved ones sang and I blew out a forest of candles. Then it was time for my favorite part. There were four gifts on the green tablecloth. I couldn't wait to unwrap them and find out the ways my family would say, "I love you." However, as I opened each gift, I really got more than I bargained for. Besides the sentiments, those gifts turned out to be an object lesson I have never forgotten.

A Gift to Acknowledge

The first gift was from my mother. It was predictable—a five-dollar check was tucked inside a pretty card. Every year without fail, Mama made sure she timed her trip to the post office perfectly so her special gift would arrive on November 21 or before.

I smiled as I read her note and tucked the check back inside the card. *Mama doesn't know a lot about inflation,* I thought. Though I had been away from home for thirty-one years, Mama's gift was always the same. I could count on it. I took it for granted. Mama may not be too creative, but she certainly is dependable.

Like the card I received faithfully from Mama, God's gifts arrive with comforting regularity. Often we take them for granted: health, friends, talents, nourishment. The Bible says that we've been given all we need for life and godliness.

God has given each of you some special abilities: be sure to use them to help each other, passing on to others God's many kinds of blessings. Are you called to preach? Then preach as though God himself were speaking through you. Are you called to help others? Do it with all the strength and energy that God supplies, so that God will be glorified through Jesus Christ — to Him be the glory and power forever and ever. Amen (1 Peter 4:10,11, TLB).

Can God Believe Me?

The second gift was from my husband. It was a box wrapped with bright yellow paper and tied with a satin bow. I could hardly wait. I picked it up and shook it. It felt like stationery. *No,* I dismissed the thought. *After thirty-one years of marriage . . . I've given the best years of my life to this man . . .* I smiled at David as I untied the bow.

Guess what? As I admired the pink flowers on the letterhead and the little blue ribbon around the envelopes, I remembered the words I had spoken just two weeks ago.

It was the day I was scheduled to speak at a conference. Intimidated by the celebrity status of other speakers, I visited a dress shop for therapy. After comparing myself to a woman orator who seemed blessed with everything I lacked (poise, style — even a refined English accent), my ordinary abilities didn't seem adequate.

The Hepburn budget had no room for a new outfit so when David saw my dress, I said, "You don't have to get me a birthday present."

And you know what? He believed me.

"Thank you, Dear." I hugged the writing paper to my chest and tried to hide my disappointment. "I love it!"

When I told David not to get me a gift, he took me at my word. When I told him that I already had all I needed, he believed me.

How often do I tell the Lord I have all I need but don't really mean it? It was unhealthy comparison that made me rush out and purchase a dress I really couldn't afford. Comparison caused me to be dissatisfied with what I had.

The Holy Spirit chooses abilities and talents that will best suit each person (see 1 Corinthians 12:11-18). When I compared myself to another speaker, I felt inferior. I began to doubt my gifts.

I identify with a comic strip where a distraught teenager moans to her best friend, "I wish I had a special 'quality' like everyone else. Delta has spunk. Tiffany has beauty. You have smarts. What do I have?"

Assuringly, her friend tells her that she has plenty of the quality that best suits her: "You have lots of *ordinary*!"

The Word of God reminds me that I have all I need.

OK, Lord,
    I believe you.
    I commit to you
    that I don't need

another thing
before I step out
to serve you.
    You can take my word for it.
    I believe you have given me all I need.
Lord,
    I think I'll use this writing paper
    to send someone
    an encouraging note.

Trust His Motives

The tag on the next gift said, "Happy Birthday from your number-one son. Love, David." The package was heavy and rattled slightly when I shook it. Pulling the tape off, I anxiously tossed the ribbon on the floor and proclaimed with much simulated cheer, "Oh! A shower head!" I smiled as I realized what many mothers through the ages have experienced at gift opening times. This gift was given with mixed motives.

You see, I *live* in the bathtub! The only time you'll catch me in the shower is at junior high summer camp. I read entire books in the tub, conduct lengthy phone conversations in the tub . . . I'd even cook breakfast in the tub if my family liked poached eggs!

My dear son, on the other hand, spends more time in the shower than is humanly healthy. The persuasive power of advertising must have convinced him that we needed one of the fun shower sprayers he had seen on TV. You know, the one where all the people are laughing and grinning because their spines are tingling and their necks are relaxing?

The Bible says that every gift God gives to us is for the purpose of edifying and building up the Body of Christ. There's no mixed motive there. We can trust Him.

Trusting God's motive is important when we begin to learn how to discover and use what He has given us. A Father who has our best interests at heart would never give us a stone when what we need is bread (see Luke 11:11).

It is not my purpose to go into a detailed description of spiritual gifts. However, I do feel that it's important for each of us to "unwrap" with discernment the gifts and abilities we've been given.

If we do, we'll learn to trust the discretion of the Holy Spirit and understand His selfless motives.

David Hocking talks about three simple keys that every believer can use to determine his or her spiritual gifts.[1]

The first key is *desire*.

"Follow the way of love," Paul wrote, "and eagerly desire spiritual gifts" (1 Corinthians 14:1, NIV).

As you read over passages of Scripture that list spiritual gifts, which ones would you like to see developed in your life? Remember that if you delight yourself in the Lord and seek to please Him, then He is the one who has placed these desires in your heart (see Psalm 37:4).

Do you long to share biblical truths with others in a clear and practical way? Maybe you have the gift of teaching. Does your heart ache when you see the needs of distressed and hurting people? Maybe you have the gift of mercy. Are you burdened for friends and neighbors who have never heard the gospel? Perhaps you have the gift of evangelism.

The second key Dr. Hocking mentions is *joy*.

"Rejoice in the Lord always. I will say it again: Rejoice!" (Philippians 4:4, NIV)

Nehemiah was a man who had a desire. When one of his brothers told him that the wall of Jerusalem was broken down and his people were left without protection, he could think of nothing else but to get that wall rebuilt. Nehemiah obviously had the gift of mercy, among others. He devoted himself to helping the poor. Though he was appointed governor, he didn't live the life of luxury to which he was entitled. Instead he shared his supper table with hundreds of needy people.

"I never demanded the food allotted to the governor, because the demands were heavy on these people" (Nehemiah 5:18, NIV). In other words, he didn't force the poor to pay taxes. Nehemiah devoted himself to exercising his gift without any thought of personal gain. And when Nehemiah's work was finished, he left the people with a reminder that would carry them through anything. He told them, "The joy of the Lord is your strength" (8:10, NIV).

Without joy we become weak. I'm sure that when Billy Graham watches hundreds of people respond to his simple message of saving grace, he is filled with joy. What spiritual gifts bring you joy?

The last key to discovering your gift is *effectiveness*. "What gifts have you found to be effective, in terms of results and in the eyes of other believers?" Hocking asks.

Paul wrote that spiritual gifts were always given to build up the Body of Christ and so that believers would be mutually encouraged.

Why is it that he gives us these special abilities to do certain things best? It is that God's people will be equipped to do better work for him, building up the church, the body of Christ to a position of strength and maturity; until finally we all believe alike about our salvation and about our Savior, God's Son, and all become full-grown in the Lord—yes, to the point of being filled full with Christ (Ephesians 4:12,13, TLB).

When you give yourself to God's work, ask yourself these questions: What effect is my ministry having on others? Are those I serve drawn closer to Christ? Is God glorified when I perform this service? Do I feel genuine joy in knowing I'm obeying God and using my talents? If you can answer yes to these questions, then you have probably discovered one or more of your gifts.

Unwrapping spiritual gifts can be as exciting as receiving birthday party gifts with one added bonus. You can always trust the giver. His motives are pure and His gifts will fulfill your desires, make you more effective and fill you with joy!

Enjoy His Gifts

One more box was left on the table. I knew it was from Lois. It was a big package. I love big packages. This time I didn't shake it. I just held it on my lap and carefully pulled the green yarn that was lovingly fashioned into a bow. My daughter's eyes twinkled. She knew it was just what I had been wanting: something I would really enjoy.

Lois had given me a Deluxe Scrabble game. She knows I love games, especially word games. Not only did she give me my favorite game, but she also bought the one with a lazy susan and plastic grooves to keep the letter tiles from slipping. This wasn't a run-of-the-mill gift and I knew it had cost a great deal more than regular Scrabble. I'm sure it made a noticeable dent in Lois's meager earnings.

This special gift had been chosen with me in mind. My daughter knew how much I would enjoy it. She knew I would share the joy with others and that she and I would probably spend many hours together using it. And Lois had purchased it at great sacrifice.

God so loved the world that He *gave*. He gave His Son (see John 3:16). He gave life and creation. He gave salvation. The great gift giver gave, and He continues to give, showering blessings upon us in abundance.

> I can never stop thanking God for all the wonderful gifts he has given you, now that you are Christ's: he has enriched your whole life. He has helped you speak out for him and has given you a full understanding of the truth; what I told you Christ could do for you has happened! Now you have every grace and blessing; every spiritual gift and power for doing his will are yours during this time of waiting for the return of our Lord Jesus Christ (1 Corinthians 1:4-7, TLB).

God is glorified as we accept, unwrap and use our gifts.

Every year, Kathleen buys her father special gifts for his birthday and Christmas. Perhaps because he lived through the Depression years, Kathleen's dad stores things. His dresser drawers are lined with never-used sweaters, slippers, ties, socks—all being kept for that "rainy day." His daughter is disappointed when Dad doesn't wear the powder blue shirt that matches the color of his eyes or the cologne that smells so good. After all, it took time, thought and money to pick out just the right gifts for him.

Imagine yourself spending hours selecting the

perfect gift for a child or grandchild. You anticipate his joy as the day approaches where Johnny will open that special something he's been longing for. Now imagine your disappointment if he were to say, "I'm not going to open this, Mom. I don't deserve it," or "I'll open it some other day. I'm too busy now."

Lois had dancing eyes when I opened my Deluxe Scrabble game. Her joy escalated when I spread out the game board and said, "C'mon, let's play right now!"

"God has given us all things richly to enjoy" (1 Timothy 6:17).

When we enjoy His gifts we are affirming His wisdom and power. We are giving God glory by saying, "Yes, Lord, you have chosen the perfect gift for me!"

God doesn't give gifts as a burden. They are meant to increase our enjoyment. They are chosen to fit our unique personality and to fulfill our calling as Christians.

The Long Walk

One of the reasons I considered my daughter's birthday present so special was that she had purchased it at great sacrifice. When God gave us the gift of His only Son, it was part of His long-term plan to provide all we need. Eternal life is a priceless gift, but there is much more.

After speaking at a women's retreat on the subject of gifts, a dear Oriental lady gave me a beautifully scripted parchment with Chinese symbols that told the tale of a gift and sacrifice.

It's an old Chinese story about a man who was separated from a beloved friend. The man longed to see his friend and wanted to present to him a gift that would show his deep esteem. But it was a day when thieves and robbers ruled the plains. Any precious gift of gold or silver would be stolen. Even paper was considered dear, so he couldn't write a letter for fear it would be taken.

One morning as he pondered the dilemma, a rare and beautiful bird perched in a nearby tree.

"Oh, I will take one of his lovely feathers as a gift! Thieves will find no value in it and it will be light to carry and easily hidden."

So the man plucked a colorful feather from the rare bird and tucked it inside his kimono, close to his heart. Then he began to make the long and painful journey of 1000 miles. On the way, he was beaten and searched repeatedly, but none of the robbers confiscated his precious gift.

His friend was overwhelmed when he received his gift, and said, "My good and faithful friend, how can I accept such a rare cumshaw (gift)? You have endured much pain and journeyed many miles."

With great devotion in his eyes, the Chinese gentleman replied, "Long walk, my friend, is part of gift."

What We Give Back

We are involved in a great gift exchange with the giver of life. He, at great sacrifice, prepared everything we need for life and godliness. The preparation is just as much a part of the gift as the presentation.

The way we respond by accepting, unwrapping and using what we have received is our gift back to

Him. Just think! When we serve in His power, then God's glory is revealed.

When the routine of our service becomes dull and our term of office seems endless, remember . . . the long walk is part of the gift.

I Protest!

If you are reproached for being Christ's followers, that
is a great privilege, for you can be sure that God's
Spirit of glory is resting upon you . . . If he suffers as a
Christian he has nothing to be ashamed of and may
glorify God in Christ's name (1 Peter 4:14,16, Phillips).

Turn on the TV. Put your feet up. It's time for a
realistic new game show titled, "Life's Unfair!" (No
one wins any prizes.)

Do you ever eat out with a friend who orders
lasagna, cherry pie a la mode, a chocolate shake—and
she wears size 3? You, in misery, have melba toast,
one lettuce leaf, black coffee, and still your bathroom
scales flash "danger zone." Metabolism just isn't fair.

Does the line you're in always move slower? Is
your permanent temporary? The repairman never
saw a model like yours? Leak-proof seals do, fail-safe
solutions aren't and, after walking to work today, you
found your dress was caught in your pantyhose?

Something I've always wanted to protest: When I
was in high school, the short cheerleaders walked
away with the basketball players! I'm 5-feet-9-inches.
It's my firm conviction that tall guys should be left for
tall gals! Life's just not fair.

I know a mother who woke at dawn, prayed, packed lunches and baked fresh cookies for after-school snacks daily. Her children ran away to a commune while a jetsetter's kids became missionaries. It's not fair.

Jan supported her husband through college. It seemed like an equitable arrangement. She worked part time, raised three children and kept the house tidy. Finally it appeared that pressures would be relieved. Tim set up a medical practice and Jan was anticipating the enjoyment of what they had both earned, when suddenly he left her for a younger woman.

Can life be fair when a child is born with deformities? My beautiful niece had a brain tumor and lived only five short months while my aged aunt lingered years in a nursing home. Suffering certainly isn't fair.

Glory Through Inequity

Adversity seems unjust. But the sovereign God says, "I can be revealed through your life, as you submit to inequities and reflect my character in how you choose to respond."

We can go through pain or we can grow through it. Troubles can distress us or bless us. It's our choice. In Hebrews 12 we read that hardships produce a harvest of righteousness and peace if we choose to be trained by them (see verse 11).

Jesus said, "In the world you will have tribulation" (John 16:33, RSV). That's a promise we don't often claim.

I received this letter from a remarkable woman who has known anguish and made a choice:

Dear Daisy,

My athletic, handsome forty-six-year-old husband was tragically electrocuted. Amazingly, he lived. However, he lost both legs, his left arm, the use of his right arm and eventually his eyesight.

I prayed each day for strength—for myself, my husband and the doctors. The Lord provided, bountifully! We made it through each day and Roy became active and content for several years.

Then cancer exploded in his body, leading to surgery and painful therapy. Total recovery never arrived. Total acceptance did. Then a careless driver took the life of our beautiful son.

Again, the Lord gave strength. Five years later, Roy went to heaven. I was left with pain, loneliness, exhaustion and other negative feelings. But through God's Word and Christian friends, I learned that grace is truly sufficient for all our needs! I don't know where my path will go from here—I just know that the Lord holds my hand and will walk each step with me . . . as I allow Him to.

I have met so many of God's wonderful people and collected precious pieces of life, and examples of Christ's love through my suffering.

I love you,

June

Tribulation is not without purpose or plan. God allows suffering so that we may refresh others, rely on Him and reveal Jesus Christ. But we have to choose to receive His comfort. There is no reason sufficient for affliction if we have not first received His gift of eternal life.

Refreshment

The Father of compassion comforts us in all our

troubles so that we can refresh and comfort others. "For just as the sufferings of Christ flow over into our lives, so also through Christ our comfort overflows" (2 Corinthians 1:3-5, NIV).

Lucy is a small, unassuming woman in her 40s. Her husband was drowned in a diving accident in the Pacific Ocean. Lucy came to our church seeking comfort. As a nurse at a San Francisco hospital, she spent time working with AIDS patients. Instead of allowing the unfairness of her experience to produce resentment in her heart, she began reaching out.

Filled with compassion, Lucy ministered to wasting bodies and hungry spirits. As she did so she saw another need. Relatives and loved ones would often come from as far as Michigan and Florida, uprooted from their homes, uncertain of how long they would need to stay, unaware of any help available to them. Because of the stigma attached to the disease, they would be confused, not knowing where to turn.

Lucy could have said, "It's not my problem. I have my own anguish to deal with." But instead she prayed for an idea. She negotiated with the administration of a private school and secured some of the empty rooms there. She has made herself available to those in need, finding them places to stay and refreshing their weary souls in the unfairness of life.

I often go kicking and screaming into trials of any kind. Lucy taught me, in her gentle way, that sorrow prepares me to identify with others' burdens. Refreshing others is one reason God allows suffering, but that's not a good enough reason to go through pain. There's got to be more to it than that.

Reliance

Comforting the afflicted is a high calling, but Paul names a second reason for suffering: "Indeed our hearts felt the sentence of death. But this happened that we might not rely on ourselves but on God" (2 Corinthians 1:9, NIV).

I believe that suffering is relative. What represents deep distress for one might be a toothache while to someone else suffering is the loss of a spouse. Christians can play a comparison game with one another and insinuate that only the deepest sufferings are worthy of God's attention.

"I had an awful headache all week. I think I'm coming down with the flu," a friend tells you.

"Well, for pity's sake," you respond. "If your problems were all I had, I'd be just fine. You should hear what I've got to deal with!"

World assistance programs have exposed the suffering of those existing in squalor without food. Some despair from the inability to make their MasterCard payment each month.

Lewis Smedes, professor of theology and ethics at Fuller Seminary, has a simple definition of suffering:

> To suffer is to put up with things you very much want not to put up with . . . Suffering can be a physical pain, like a headache or bone cancer. It can be mental anguish, like the desperate loneliness that sets in when a loved one dies . . . What marks any human experience as suffering, and what binds us together in a fraternity of sufferers, is a powerful desire that our pain, our grief, our hurt go away, and we have no power to make it go.[1]

What constitutes suffering, the Bible gives us no freedom to compare.

Corrie ten Boom learned to respond to the inequities of life at an early age. In *Corrie ten Boom: Her Life, Her Faith,*[2] this story is told.

In 1917 Corrie was living in her parental home in Haarlem, Holland, when a fine young man came into her life.

This must be the one God has for me! Corrie thought. She longed to make a good home for a godly husband. Karel and Corrie would take long walks through the countryside talking about his call to the ministry and their ambitions for the future.

Karel went to seminary and the day Corrie received word that he was coming home was an exciting one. She put on her best dress and prepared a meal. Her mama cleaned the house and her papa put on a suit. When the doorbell rang, everything was perfect.

Corrie whisked it open and there stood her beloved with a fashionable girl on his arm.

"Corrie, I'd like you to meet my fiancee," he said.

Crushed and disheartened, Corrie could have chosen anger and bitterness. Why did he deceive her? Why had God allowed her to look so foolish?

Instead, she reasoned, *If I, knowing Christ, feel distressed, what must be going on with young women who lack faith?*

Gathering up girls who needed a friend, Corrie started Girls' Guides (comparable to Pioneer Clubs) throughout Holland. "Seek your strength through prayer" was the club motto.

Not only did Corrie rely on God, she taught

others to rely on Him. Corrie was being prepared for suffering on a far deeper level. One day it would alter her life forever. She refreshed others, relied upon God and automatically demonstrated a third reason God allows unfairness to befall Christians.

Revelation

Christ is revealed through difficulties.

He has delivered us from such a deadly peril, and he will deliver us. On him we have set our hope that he will continue to deliver us, as you help us by your prayers. Then many will give thanks on our behalf for the gracious favor granted us in answer to the prayers of many (2 Corinthians 1:10,11, NIV).

Many will give thanks when they see God at work in the tornado of tribulation. Do you know anyone who lives so victoriously that you can't help saying, "If God can do that for her, then I can trust Him for what I am going through"?

A missionary woman, home on furlough from the Philippines, was kidnapped and held hostage for fifty-two days. Though the experience was terrifying, she felt that God used it for His glory.

In a magazine article she was quoted as saying, "People tell me that they can go through some kinds of trouble now because they see that the resources God gave me are available to them, too. They see that I'm not a super saint. I'm just like them. God gave me strength, and He will give strength to them."

The gift of strength in the midst of crisis is God's glory displayed.

In a long-ago display of glory, a man stood silent, staring into the Atlantic Ocean. Storm clouds rumbled and wave upon wave crashed against jagged rocks as constant agony threatened to overwhelm him.

Horatio Spafford's only son was dead. On top of that, the Chicago Fire of 1871 had wiped out his business and sent him to the brink of financial ruin. Seeking reprieve from the grief, Spafford's wife and four daughters sailed for Great Britain where he was planning to join them. Well-known evangelist D. L. Moody was holding a campaign in Britain and the family looked forward to spiritual refreshment that would surely nourish their hungry souls.

But on November 22, 1873, their plans were cruelly cut off. The S. S. Ville du Havre, the ship his family occupied, was struck by an English vessel and sank in twelve minutes. There were few survivors and his daughters were not among them.

A cable from Mrs. Spafford, who had been taken to Wales to recover, simply read, "Saved alone."

His grief was great, but his God was greater, and as Horatio G. Spafford wiped the salt water mist and the hot tears from his face, something beyond agony stirred deep within. These words formed on his lips:

> When peace, like a river, attendeth my way,
> When sorrows like sea billows roll
> Whatever my lot, Thou has taught me to say,
> It is well, it is well with my soul.
>
> Tho Satan should buffet, tho trials should come.
> Let this blest assurance control,
> That Christ hath regarded my helpless estate,
> And hath shed His own blood for my soul.[3]

It is well, it is well with my soul. Imagine the scores of believers who have mouthed the melody of that great hymn and given thanks. Glory radiates when we submit and accept. When we let God be God.

When we choose not to shake clenched fists and cry, "Why me, Lord?" but to open our hands and say, "Whatever, Lord, if this will gain you greater glory."

Glory in Suffering

How can the unfairness of life glorify God?

"Suffering is a touchstone in human experience," says Margaret Clarkson, another hymn writer who has known suffering through illness and loneliness. "If we can glorify Him there, we are likely to be able to glorify Him anywhere."

She suggests at least four things that happen when a Christian responds with patience, gentleness and faithfulness to the inequities of life:

1. God's holiness and power are displayed.

2. Christ's victory is vindicated.

3. Satan is rebuked and cast down.

4. The sufferers are glorified as God forms His life more clearly in them.[4]

It's not in our nature to respond that way, but if we are to share God's glory, we must also share His suffering (see Romans 8:17).

Before Corrie ten Boom died in 1983 at the age of ninety-two, she had traveled all over the world telling of the glorious power of Jesus Christ. Hers was an exciting, fruitful ministry. But the fruit came out of the horror she experienced while confined in Ravensbruck, reportedly the worst of the Nazi concentration camps.

"My message all over the world has been that

even in the darkest pit of despair, Jesus is always with us," Corrie said. "I know. I was there."

Life is unfair. Bad things happen to good people. Storm clouds brew over the just and the unjust. But if we choose to respond to life's inequities by comforting others, depending on God and displaying His gentle nature, we can touch hope.

We can sing softly: "It is well, it is well with my soul."

You're Welcome

He who practices thank offerings honors me, and he
prepares the way so that I may show him the salvation
of God (Psalm 50:23, NIV).

We were seated at the supper table on a dreary
October evening in our home at Mount Hermon. The
whole day had been foggy and drippy. My husband
and I were joined by two little neighbor girls who
often graced our table these days. Their mama had
gone through the most traumatic year of her life.
Among other things, her husband had walked out,
leaving her with the overwhelming responsibility of
supporting their daughters.

As I was spooning potatoes onto Jessica's plate,
the sun came bursting through the clouds in time for
us to watch it set over the mountains and the Pacific
Ocean. It was brilliant and colorful, coming just at the
point when we had become acclimated to the
dreariness of that day. A beautiful sunset in the midst
of that dark fog had seemed unlikely.

"Oh, thank you, Jesus, for the sunshine!" I
remarked and went on serving.

About thirty seconds went by and we were into
another part of the conversation when five-year-old

Jessica looked up at me with her big brown eyes and whispered, "Daisy . . . Daisy?"

I smoothed a napkin out on my lap and leaned over, "What is it, Honey?"

"Daisy," she answered softly, "He said . . . *You're welcome.*"

How I needed that reminder.

Sometimes we forget to see things from God's perspective — with a grateful heart. Sometimes we forget to stop and listen for His still, small voice. Sometimes we only thank Him for the sunshine.

Circumstances are allowed or even sent into our lives so that we may be more exquisitely conformed to the image of the Son of God.

A little boy asked a wood carver, "How do you carve a horse?"

"Well, Son, you just knock off everything that doesn't look like a horse!"

From our perspective, it often seems like there will be no respite from life's clouds. The "knocking off" process seems to go on forever as we are shaped into His image. But if we can come to the point in our lives where we're able to say:

Thank you, Jesus.

Thank you for this family member
    who's not the easiest person
    in the world to live with.

Thank you for this body,
    consumed by infirmity.

Thank you for the responsibilities
    of this busy schedule
    when I don't think I can cope another
        minute.

Lord,
>Thank you for every circumstance
>surrounding my life,
>for every experience
>You have woven into the fabric
>of my days.

The sun will break through. Then listen closely and you'll hear Him say: "You're welcome, dear one. You're very welcome."

We spent four years in lovely Puerto Rico. One of the things I learned to tolerate was constant, unexpected, tropical rain showers. At first, I considered it a nuisance. If we were having a backyard Bible club, our crafts were spoiled. If I had just had my hair done, I was instantly transformed to the wet-mop look. Eventually, however, we learned to behave like the natives. We didn't even bother with umbrellas but went on about our business and pretended it wasn't happening. Soon, I became grateful for refreshing rain and the lush greenery it produced.

One day, our seven-year-old son came running into the house and said, "Mama, Mama, come quick and look!"

I followed him outside and saw something I had never seen before and have never seen since. In the sky above us was the complete circle of a rainbow! It was as if God had carefully placed a halo of color above His creation. It made me think of the contrast between God's view and our own.

We see our world blackened with sin and its consequences. Often, from our perspective, it doesn't look all that good. But God sees everything through the prism of His love. He mixes rain with sunshine.

And the result is the awesome beauty of His design on creation's canvas.

I'm so grateful to live on this side of Calvary. Because of who Jesus is, you and I can say, "Thank you, Lord, that we're part of the blood-washed church." God sees us through the righteousness of Jesus Christ, through the rainbow of His love.

I don't know what the Lord has promised you or what He has delivered to you this year, this week, this day. But I do know that learning to see our lives from God's perspective with gratitude for what He has allowed—or sent—will make a crucial difference. How you receive the fulfillment of His promises in your life can make you a victim or a victor.

Joni Eareckson Tada visited Corrie ten Boom one day shortly before Corrie went to heaven. Corrie had suffered several strokes and was confined to a wheelchair, paralyzed. Joni, too, lives in a wheelchair because of a diving accident that left her a quadriplegic. Joni and Corrie talked and prayed, and Joni sang.

"I felt our mutual weakness," Joni said. "Yet I am certain neither of us had ever felt stronger."[1]

The secret of their strength and joy is something that's available to everyone. It is the *ability to glorify God with a thankful heart*. Joni refuses to waste life on despair and regret. Infirmity has brought her closer to her Savior. Thus, she views her circumstance as an incomparable gift. She has chosen thankfulness as a way of life when she could have chosen bitterness.

"He who sacrifices thank offerings [glorifies] me, and he prepares the way so that I may show him the salvation of God" (Psalm 50:23, NIV).

Sometimes giving thanks is a sacrifice.

By April of 1621, over half of the people who struggled to journey from England on the Mayflower had died. Harsh winter weather took its toll and the little band of Pilgrims must have wondered if the God they worshiped had deserted them. Some wanted to turn back. But after much discussion, they decided to trust and wait. As the first anniversary of the Mayflower's landing approached, they began to plan a remembrance.

But how would they acknowledge that day? How would they receive the unfair blows that had torn them apart and broken their hearts? Some wanted to have a day of mourning. After all, fifty-two graves were a reminder of their sorrow and loss. Following lengthy deliberation and prayer, they realized that even though there was much to grieve about, there was also much to be thankful for.

They were free. They were blessed with good harvests, good friends and a good, hopeful future. They chose to sift through the circumstances that had befallen them and give glory to God with an annual sacrifice of thanksgiving. They focused on gratitude. Don't you wonder what the last Thursday in November would be like for us every year if they had chosen to mourn instead? Do you think the attitude of our Puritan forefathers shaped our nation? I do.

"I will praise God's name in song and glorify him with thanksgiving" (Psalm 69:30, NIV).

I have mentioned in previous chapters that to glorify God means to reveal His character. When we have a thankful heart, God's loving nature is displayed in our lives.

On the morning that I was getting ready to fly

from California to Pennsylvania to say good-bye to my
mama for the last time, I picked up a devotional book
from the stand beside my bed. Amy Carmichael's
words were more than appropriate as I thought about
Mama going to heaven.

> For the love that, like a screen,
> sheltered from the might-have-been,
>   be Thy Name adored.[2]

After reading that thought, I wrote in my
notebook: *If you can't thank God for what you've
received, thank Him for what you've been spared.*

Throughout the day I thought about all that
God's love had protected me from and I offered up a
deep prayer of thanksgiving for my parents who were
used by the Lord to shelter me from the
might-have-beens. I am a privileged character.

"I believe our whole life — everything we
do — should be toward the one goal of glorifying God,"
a co-worker remarked to another Christian at the
office one day. "People in this office don't give the
Lord a thought. So, it's up to us to demonstrate His
power."

Mab Hoover was convicted.

"Lord," she prayed, "this is serious. What can I
do to bring glory to you?"

Immediately Luke 8:39 came into her mind:
"Tell how much God has done for you" (NIV).

Verbalize thanksgiving. Someone said that silent
gratitude isn't much use to anyone.

At a weekend retreat, women shared:

"I was a victim of child abuse."

"My father was an alcoholic."

"The Lord saved me from suicide."

And when an unbeliever heard the testimonies from their thankful hearts, she wanted to meet their Savior.

I was raised by godly parents whose role-modeling was so convincing I wanted nothing more than to serve Christ with gladness. My thank offering is that I had a mother and father who prayed for me every day of my life. I love to tell what God has done for me.

"Daddy? This is Daisy," I yelled into the receiver. Daddy's hearing was failing in the last weeks of his life.

"Who?" he shouted. And I'm sure every resident of the convalescent home heard him.

"*Daisy!*"

"Oh," Daddy replied, and I could hear his voice crack, "my boy!"

Daddy had called me his boy from the day I was born. I was the fourth in a line of five daughters. Often he would tell people as he tussled my hair playfully, "This is the boy I prayed for. You see how the Lord answered my prayer! He just said NO!"

"My Boy?" Daddy said softer now in that final phone conversation. "I'm praying for you. And, Boy?"

"Yes, Daddy?"

"Don't be surprised if the Lord comes to get me pretty soon. I want you to know . . . I'm ready . . . I'm ready."

"Oh, Daddy. I am, too."

I'm privileged and I'm thankful to be a daughter of godly parents. As the seasons of life converge, I offer the Lord my thankful heart. Thirty years ago in

San Francisco I received a phone call that changed my life forever.

"Mrs. Hepburn?" I recognized the voice on the other end and my eyes filled as I listened to words I had longed to hear.

"Mrs. Hepburn, you have a son."

How I thank God for a woman I have never met who chose to give birth to her baby boy; she allowed me the honor of being a mother.

I thank the Lord that this son is fulfilling God's goals for his life (one of which is to keep his mother right where she belongs—on her knees!).

I say, "Thank you, Lord, for this son," and I think there's a smile on His face when He says, "You're welcome."

Four years later, we received another phone call and raced to pick up our thirty-six-hour-old baby girl.

I thank the Lord that David and Lois have made such an impact on my life as agents of accountability. There's nothing that calls me to holy living like the fact that my son and daughter have the God-given right to follow my example. Whether we like it or not, mothers are role-models. We're constantly teaching our children something about life.

A woman whose parents had died from alcoholism said that for years she searched for a mentor, someone who would say, "Follow me. I'll teach you right from wrong."

She never found anyone, but her life was transformed when, one day, she prayed, "Lord, make *me* a role model."

One way I have found to model faith and thanksgiving to our children was suggested by a woman I met at a conference I was attending. Each year Margaret would purchase a new Bible. Throughout the year she would read the entire sixty-six books with one of her seven grandchildren in mind, making notations, tucking prayer cards and bookmarks in, praying daily for that one. At the end of the year she would give the Bible as a gift to the child.

I can't tell you what a blessing it has been these past years as I am doing the same for David and Lois and their spouses.

We can have an influence on our families for generations to come, if we cultivate gratitude to God for all He has done. Faye Field is a woman who was impacted by a grandmother she never even met, nearly 150 years after that godly woman went to glory.

Grandma Sarah Alice Germany lived on a farm in Texas. One day Faye's cousin brought an old tattered Bible to Faye and said, "I want you to have this."

At first, Faye was less than thrilled. But after examining it she began to notice marginal notations that her grandmother had made.

Beside Genesis 41:9 it read: "I talked sharply to Jackie today. Forgive me."

"Nov. 18, 1879—I got discouraged today. I forgot how much I have already," was penned by Deuteronomy 2:7.

Near Exodus 34:2, which says, "Be ready in the morning," Grandma Sarah wrote, "Lord, I'm ready at 4 A.M."

On and on the notations, prayers and praises went all the way through the New Testament. Faye was encouraged and strengthened in her own faith as she realized the eternal power of God's Word.

I bring God a thank offering today that I am a mother and mother-in-love. "Thank you, Lord, for these children."

Can you hear Him answer? "You're welcome."

Thirty-seven years ago, David Hepburn and I lifted a verse from a promise box. It suited us so well, we had it inscribed in our wedding rings. I've never had mine off, but when I'm thinner, I can pinch the skin on my knuckle and read it: "This God is our God forever and ever and He will be our guide even unto death" (Psalm 48:14, KJV).

How I thank God that I am the wife of a man who is committed to Christ. Through financial pressure, parental pressure, ministry pressure and now the biggest challenge of his life, as he administers a Christian high school in San Francisco, David has served the Lord with gladness.

Thank you, Jesus. I am the wife of a man who is trusting you even today, for whatever you have ahead of us . . . and I'm listening.

I want to glorify God with a thankful heart for all I have been given and all I have been spared.

And my Lord says, "You're welcome. You're very welcome."

Glory Be!

Dear Lord,

We sang the old hymn today
> "In the cross of Christ I glory
> Towering o'er the wrecks of time;
> All the light of sacred story
> Gathers round its head sublime."

I remember Paul's fervency:
> "God forbid that I should glory
> save in the cross . . ."[1]
> I make the same request.

You have honored me
> You have humbled me
> You have been willing to "get glory through me"[2]
> You have even allowed me to be a vessel for
> "pouring your glory into"![3]

Please help me to reveal your character
> in my attitudes
> in my responses to life's inequities
> in my use of your gifts and abilities
> but especially as I learn more of what it means
> to be crucified with You

Deepening my roots in You
> reaching higher toward excellency in my
> knowledge of You
> so that the breadth of my influence
> honors You.

There is the cross again, Lord.
> Depth and breadth
> Still an instrument of death, of life.

Help me to GLORY IN THE CROSS . . .
> No—help me not to glory in anything but the cross!

> GLORY BE!
> to Thee
> through me.

Amen

Worth Looking Into

The man who simply hears and does nothing about it is like a man catching the reflection of his own face in a mirror. He sees himself, it is true, but he goes on with whatever he was doing without the slightest recollection of what sort of person he saw in the mirror. But the man who looks into the perfect mirror of God's law, the law of liberty, and makes a habit of so doing, is not the man who sees and forgets (James 1:23,24, Phillips).

But we all, with open face beholding as in a glass the glory of the Lord, are changed into the same image from glory to glory, even as by the Spirit of the Lord (2 Corinthians 3:18).

I. LOOK UP . . . and see God!

A. When you are asked to describe God's character, what comes to mind?

B. Read these Scriptures and list what they reveal about God's character qualities.

Psalm 103:1-18   Isaiah 40:28-31

Psalm 145:8-21   Romans 8:31,32

Psalm 146   Revelation 4:11

C. Which of these characteristics are you most grateful for right now? Why?

II. LOOK WITHIN . . . and see yourself!

A. According to Romans 8:29 what is God's goal for your life?

B. Read 2 Corinthians 3:18 and rewrite it in your own words:

C. God is in the business of *changing us!* What changes have you experienced this year in your home, job, circumstances?

D. What changes have you experienced in your goals, your spiritual life, your attitudes, etc.?

E. Is there an area of your life that you can identify that needs *more change?*

F. Read 1 John 4:9,10. What was God's greatest expression of love?

G. If you haven't memorized John 3:16, do it right now. Close your Bible and write it here from memory.

H. Read Romans 5:6-11. What did the Father's love cause Him to do for you?

I. According to Ephesians 2:8,9, what is the free
gift offered to all mankind?

If you have received His gift of grace, thank Him
and consider the ways your life can be a new
commitment to His purposes for you. Write down
your prayer of thanksgiving:

If you have not yet received Him and His grace
for you personally, why not make this your moment to
begin a new life in harmony with His plan for your
life? Here is a suggested prayer for you to pray:

*Dear Lord Jesus, I know that I am a sinner. Please
forgive me. I believe that you died and gave yourself to
pay the price for my sins. I cannot save myself. I want to
turn from my sins and begin a new life. Right now I
invite you to come into my life as Lord and Savior. I
trust that you will begin a work of love in me and help
me to become all that you planned for me to be.*

III. LOOK AROUND . . . and see the world!

A. Read Matthew 4:3,6,9. How did Satan try to defeat Jesus?

B. Is there any correlation between Jeremiah 9:23 and the passage you just read?

C. Look up the following verses. How does each encourage us to *glorify God?* Write down some suggestions that would make each one practical to your daily living right now.

1 Peter 4:11

Matthew 5:15

Matthew 25:31-46

John 15:8

Kinds of fruit our lives are to produce:

Romans 1:13

Romans 6:21-23

Philippians 4:17

Colossians 1:9,10

Galatians 5:21,22

Hebrews 13:15

IV. Let's LOOK INTO HIS WORD!

In Ephesians 1:1-14 Paul outlines the work of the triune God.

A. What has the *Father* done?

Verse 3

Verse 4

Verse 5

Why has God the Father done all this for us?

Verse 6

B. What is the work of the *Son*?

Verse 7

Verse 8

Verse 11

Why has God the Son done this for us?

Verse 12

C. What has the *Holy Spirit* done for us?

Verse 13

Verse 14

Everything that the Father, Son and Spirit have done reveals something about God. This is so men might see what God is like by what He has done. Then they can worship, honor and praise Him. Even our salvation is designed to bring *glory to God*.

Reflect for a few moments on what God has done for you. How has God revealed Himself to you in these verses?

To this end also we pray for you always that our God may count you worthy of your calling, and fulfill every desire for goodness and the work of faith with power; in order that the name of our Lord Jesus may be glorified *in you, and you in Him, according to the grace of our God and the Lord Jesus Christ* (2 Thessalonians 1:11,12).

D. Read and enjoy Psalm 8. What spiritual sign of authority has God given you?

E. Read and enjoy Psalm 19. What is the psalmist's response to the display of *the glory of God* in creation and in His Word? Does this psalm contain a prayer you might pray to the Lord?

F. Read and enjoy Psalm 145. Do what verse 5 says to do!

G. Write a short psalm of your own, praising God for a small miracle in your life (see Psalm 145:6).

Notes

Chapter One

1. Elisabeth Elliot, *The Glory of God's Will* (Westchester, IL: Good News Publishers, 1982).

2. Grant Colfax Tullar

Chapter Two

1. Evelyn Christenson, *Lord, Change Me* (Wheaton, IL: Victor Books/Scripture Press, 1977).

Chapter Three

1. J. Dwight Pentecost, *The Glory of God* (Portland, OR: Multnomah Press, 1978), pp. 8-9.

Chapter Four

1. *The Humanist Manifesto I*, p. 8.

2. *The Humanist Manifesto II*, p. 13.

3. Taken from an advertisement by Citizens Against Pornography (CAP), July 17, 1987. For more information, write CAP, P. O. Box 506, Citrus Heights, CA 95611.

4. George Gallup, *War Cry* (February 14, 1987), p. 10.

5. Frank R. Tillapaugh, *Unleashing the Church* (Ventura, CA: Regal Books, Division of Gospel Light Publications, 1982), p. 92.

6. From the tract, "You Are Responsible" (Scottsdale, AZ: Faith American Foundation).

Chapter Five

1. Larry Christensen, *The Transformed Mind*.

Chapter Six

1. Elisabeth Elliot, *A Slow & Certain Light* (Nashville, TN: Abingdon Press, 1982), p. 67.

2. Amy Carmichael from the *I Dare* series, Child Evangelism Fellowship.

Chapter Seven

1. From an article by John J. Goldman, *The Sacramento Bee* (August 27, 1987).

2. Elaine Stedman, *Woman's Worth* (Waco, TX: Word Books, 1976).

3. Margaret Clarkson, *Destined for Glory: The Meaning of Suffering* (Grand Rapids, MI: Wm. B. Eerdmans Pub. Co., 1983).

4. Elisabeth Elliot, *Passion and Purity* (Old Tappan, NJ: Fleming H. Revell Co., 1984).

Chapter Eight

1. Adapted from a devotional in *The Daily Bread*.

2. From a Dr. James Dobson radio broadcast.

3. Used by permission.

4. Used by permission.

Chapter Nine

1. Taken from a radio broadcast.

Chapter Ten

1. Lewis Smedes, *How Can it Be All Right When Everything Is All Wrong?* (New York: Pocket Books, Div. of Simon & Schuster, n.d.).

2. Carole C. Carlson, *Corrie ten Boom: Her Life, Her Faith* (Old Tappan, NJ: Fleming H. Revell Co., 1982).

3. Kenneth W. Osbeck, *101 Hymn Stories* (Grand Rapids, MI: Kregel Publishing, 1982).

4. Margaret Clarkson, *Destined for Glory: The Meaning of Suffering* (Grand Rapids, MI: Wm. B. Eerdmans Pub. Co., 1983).

5. Carlson, *Corrie ten Boom.*

Chapter Eleven

1. Joni Eareckson Tada, *Choices* (Grand Rapids, MI: Zondervan Publishing House, 1986).

2. Amy Carmichael, *Whispers of His Love* (Old Tappan, NJ: Fleming H. Revell Co., 1982), p. 78.

Glory Be!

1. Galatians 6:14.

2. John 17:10.

3. Romans 9:23, TLB

Life-Changing Reading
for Today's Woman

Total

———— **"The Greatest Lesson I've Ever Learned,"** Vonette $ _____
Zachary Bright, editor. More than 20 prominent
Christian women share the lessons that shaped their
lives. Features Barbara Bush, Ann Kiemel Anderson,
Joni Eareckson Tada, and more!
ISBN 0-89840-286-7/hardcover/$12.95

———— **Being a Woman of God** by Ginger Gabriel. A woman's $ _____
Bible study on the qualities that result in God's
blessings and enhance personal effectiveness in a
woman. ISBN 0-86605-144-9/$4.25

———— **Where Have All the Lovers Gone?** by Pamala Condit $ _____
Kennedy. Rekindle the romance in your marriage by
becoming the woman your husband can't resist!
Hundreds of creative ideas to liven up your marriage.
ISBN 0-89840-292-1/$8.95

Your Christian bookseller should have these products in stock.
Please check with him before using this "Shop by Mail" form.

Send completed order form to: **HERE'S LIFE PUBLISHERS, INC.**
P. O. Box 1576
San Bernardino, CA 92402-1576

Name _____

Address _____

City _____ State _____ Zip _____

☐ Payment enclosed
   (check or money order only)

☐ Visa ☐ Mastercard

#_____

Expiration Date _____

Signature _____

For faster service,
call toll free:
1-800-950-4457

ORDER TOTAL	$ _____
SHIPPING and HANDLING ($1.50 for one item, $0.50 for each additional. Do not exceed $4.00.)	$ _____
APPLICABLE SALES TAX (CA 6.75%)	$ _____
TOTAL DUE	$ _____

Please allow 2 to 4 weeks for delivery.
Prices subject to change without notice.

WSG 313-8